GREEK MYTHOLOGY

A Collection of the Best Greek Myths

By
Jason Dodd

Table of Contents

Introduction

In the grand tapestry of human storytelling, few narratives are as rich, as enduring, or as profoundly influential as those found in Greek mythology. "Greek Mythology: A Collection of the Best Greek Myths" invites you on a journey through a world where the line between the divine and the mortal blurs, where heroes face unimaginable challenges, and where the machinations of gods set the fates of men and women. This book is a gateway into a realm that has captivated the imagination for thousands of years, offering a treasure trove of tales that continue to resonate with our contemporary world.

As we open this collection, we begin by introducing you to the foundational beings of Greek mythology—the Titans. These primordial figures emerge from the chaos of creation to forge the universe as we know it. Their stories are not only tales of power and conflict but also of the elemental forces that shape our world.

Following the Titans, we ascend to Mount Olympus with Chapter 2, where the Olympians reign. Here, gods and goddesses like Zeus, Hera, Athena, and Apollo navigate a world rife with passion, intrigue, and power struggles, often mirroring the complexities of human emotions and relationships.

In Chapter 3, we delve into the lives of other significant characters populating these myths. From cunning nymphs to brave mortals, these figures add depth and nuance to the mythological landscape, showcasing the breadth of themes Greek mythology encompasses.

Chapter 4 brings us to the very genesis of the world—the Creation Myth. This narrative sets the stage for understanding the ancient Greek worldview, a cosmos where chaos gives way to order, and where from darkness comes light.

The Titanomachy, covered in Chapter 5, recounts the epic battle for supremacy between the old gods and the new, a tale that is as much about the struggle for power as it is about the inevitable passage of time and the rise of new generations.

From Chapter 6 onwards, we immerse ourselves in a selection of the most celebrated and enduring stories from Greek mythology. The twelve labors of Heracles, the tragic tale of Echo and Narcissus, the cunning Prometheus, the curious Pandora, and the harrowing abduction of Persephone are recounted with a focus on their enduring themes and lessons.

The book continues with the legendary adventures of Theseus and the Minotaur, the ingenious Daedalus and his ill-fated son Icarus, the heroic Perseus and his battle with the Gorgon Medusa, and concludes with the poignant story of King Midas, who learned about the true value of his golden touch.

This collection, "Greek Mythology: A Collection of the Best Greek Myths," is more than a mere recounting of ancient tales. It is an exploration of the human condition, a reflection on themes like love and hate, loyalty and betrayal, ambition and failure, and the constant quest for understanding and meaning. As you journey through these pages, you are invited to explore a world where myths are not just stories but windows into the deepest aspects of human nature, culture, and belief.

Welcome to the world of Greek mythology, where each myth is a path to understanding the timeless narratives that continue to shape our world. Let us embark on this journey together, with the turn of each page opening a new chapter in the eternal saga of the gods.

Chapter 1: The Titans

In Greek mythology, there were originally twelve Titans, six males and six females, who were the children of the primordial deities Uranus (Sky) and Gaia (Earth). These twelve Titans are often referred to as the first generation of Titans. In this chapter, we will introduce you to these Titan gods and goddesses.

Cronus (Kronos)

Cronus, also known as Kronos, is a central figure in Greek mythology, known primarily as the leader of the Titans and the father of several of the Olympian gods. He is a deity of time, particularly in its destructive aspect as an all-devouring force. In myth, Cronus is the son of Uranus (the Sky) and Gaia (the Earth). Fearing a prophecy that he would be overthrown by one of his children, just as he had overthrown his own father, Cronus swallowed each of his offspring as they were born. This act of consuming his children is one of his most defining and horrifying characteristics.

Cronus's reign was considered a Golden Age on Earth, a time of prosperity and happiness that ended with his overthrow. His wife, the Titaness Rhea, deceived him to save their youngest child, Zeus, by giving Cronus a stone wrapped in swaddling clothes to swallow instead of the baby. Zeus was raised in secret and eventually challenged Cronus, leading to the Titanomachy, a great war between the Titans, led by Cronus, and the Olympians, led by Zeus. After the defeat of the Titans, Cronus was imprisoned in Tartarus, or, in some versions of the myth, became the king of Elysium, a paradise for the righteous and heroic souls.

Cronus is often conflated with the Roman god Saturn, inheriting many of his attributes and festivals. The themes surrounding Cronus often include the cycles of time, the inevitability of fate, and the transition of power from generation to generation. His story sets the stage for the rise of the Olympian gods and the establishment of a new order in the cosmos, representing a shift from the old, primal forces embodied by the Titans to the more structured and civilized reign of the Olympians.

Rhea

Rhea is a significant figure in Greek mythology, known as the Titaness daughter of the earth goddess Gaia and the sky god Uranus. She is often associated with fertility, motherhood, and generation. Rhea is most famous for her role as the wife of Cronus, the leader of the Titans, and the mother of the first generation of Olympian gods, including Zeus, Hades, Poseidon, Hera, Demeter, and Hestia.

Her most notable myth involves her role in saving her youngest son, Zeus, from being swallowed by Cronus. Cronus, having usurped Uranus, feared a prophecy that he would be overthrown by one of his own children. To prevent this, he swallowed each of his offspring at birth. When Zeus was born, Rhea sought to save him by substituting a stone wrapped in swaddling clothes for the infant god, which Cronus swallowed, thinking it was his son. Rhea then hid Zeus in a cave on Crete, where he was raised and eventually grew strong enough to challenge and defeat Cronus, leading to the ascendancy of the Olympian gods.

Rhea's character embodies the maternal archetype in Greek mythology. She is often depicted as a motherly figure, riding a chariot pulled by lions. Her connection to the earth and nature is significant, reflecting the ancient Greeks' reverence for the nurturing aspects of the earth and the cycles of life and fertility. While not as prominently featured in myths as her children, Rhea's role as the mother of key

Olympian gods and her actions to protect Zeus were crucial in the transition of power from the Titans to the Olympians, marking a significant shift in Greek mythological history.

Oceanus

In Greek mythology, Oceanus is a Titan, son of the primordial deities Uranus (Sky) and Gaia (Earth). He represents the vast, unbounded waters that encircled the flat earth, known as the "world-ocean." As a primordial entity, Oceanus is a personification of the sea itself, distinct from Poseidon, the later Olympian god of the sea. He is often depicted as a serene and benevolent figure, in contrast to the more tempestuous sea gods.

Oceanus's role in Greek myth is relatively passive and backgrounded compared to other deities, yet his presence is foundational. He is often referred to as the father of all waters and is associated with every aspect of the sea, from the calmest pool to the furthest reaches of the ocean. Oceanus and his sister-wife, Tethys, are said to have parented the rivers of the world (known as the Potamoi), as well as the three-thousand ocean nymphs (the Oceanids). This vast progeny signifies the interconnectedness of all water bodies in the ancient Greeks' conception of the world.

In art and literature, Oceanus is frequently depicted as an old man with a long beard and crab-claw horns, often with the lower body of a serpent. He appears in a few mythological stories, but he is best known for his representation of the world's waters and his genealogical importance as the forebear of all water deities and entities. Oceanus symbolizes the mysterious, life-giving, and boundless nature of water, an element essential to Greek life and culture.

Tethys

Tethys, in Greek mythology, is a Titaness and the daughter of the primordial deities Uranus (Sky) and Gaia (Earth). She is the sister and wife of Oceanus, the god of the world-ocean, and together they represent the sea's divine aspects. Tethys, as a goddess, personifies the fresh water that feeds the earth, encompassing rivers, springs, streams, and rain clouds. This role as a nurturer of the earth's waters reflects the ancient Greeks' understanding of the water cycle and its critical importance to life and agriculture.

Tethys's most prominent role in mythology is as the mother of the numerous river gods, known as the Potamoi, and the three thousand Oceanids, nymphs who represent everything from bodies of water to various natural phenomena and qualities. This vast and varied progeny highlights her status as a maternal figure and her association with the life-giving aspects of water. Despite her importance as a mother figure and a water deity, Tethys does not feature prominently in many myths or stories. Instead, her significance is more symbolic, representing the fecund and nurturing aspects of nature.

In artistic depictions, Tethys is often portrayed as a matronly woman, sometimes with attributes that reflect her association with water, such as shells or water-themed adornments. She symbolizes the critical role of water in sustaining life, both in terms of physical nourishment and agricultural fertility. Tethys, much like her husband Oceanus, represents the Greeks' reverence for and understanding of the natural world's essential and sustaining elements.

Hyperion

Hyperion, in Greek mythology, is one of the twelve Titan children of Gaia (Earth) and Uranus (Sky). His name often translates to "he who goes above" or "the high one," signifying his role as the Titan of light and celestial phenomena. As a primordial figure, Hyperion embodies the aspects of light and heavenly bodies, particularly the sun and the moon, contributing to the creation of day and night, the seasons, and time itself.

Hyperion's most significant role in mythology comes from his offspring. He married his sister, Theia, and they became the parents of Helios (the Sun), Selene (the Moon), and Eos (the Dawn). Through his children, Hyperion is intricately connected to the daily rhythm of life in Greek thought, influencing everything from agriculture to navigation and religious rituals. His son Helios is often depicted driving the chariot of the sun across the sky, marking the passage of day, while Selene does the same for the moon, controlling the night.

Despite his fundamental role in the cosmic order, Hyperion does not feature prominently in many myths. Like many of the Titans, his presence is more foundational than active in the stories that constitute the bulk of Greek mythology. The mythological focus shifts to his children, especially Helios, who took on a more personified and active role in later myths and cults. Hyperion's legacy is thus more about his contribution to the creation and maintenance of the natural world's order, symbolizing the omnipresent and vital force of light in the ancient Greeks' understanding of the world.

Theia

Theia, in Greek mythology, is a Titaness, daughter of the primordial deities Uranus (Sky) and Gaia (Earth). She represents the very essence of brightness and shining, often associated with the luminosity of the sky, the glimmer of precious metals, and the brilliance of the eyes. Theia's role in Greek myths is less about her individual exploits and more about her contribution to the cosmic order through her offspring.

Married to her brother Hyperion, another Titan, Theia is the mother of Helios (the Sun), Selene (the Moon), and Eos (the Dawn). This lineage is crucial in ancient Greek cosmology, as her children are responsible for significant celestial phenomena. Helios traverses the sky daily, marking the passage of time with his sun chariot. Selene, likewise, controls the phases of the moon, influencing various aspects of life and mythology. Eos, representing the dawn, brings the light of day to the world each morning.

Theia's contribution through her children reflects the ancient Greeks' reverence for the natural order and the celestial bodies that govern it. Although Theia herself does not feature prominently in many stories, her presence is felt through the daily and nightly reminders of her progeny. In artistic depictions, she is sometimes shown in the company of her children, symbolizing her connection to light and vision. Theia embodies the beauty and power of light, an essential force in the world of the ancient Greeks, both practically and symbolically.

Coeus

Coeus, in Greek mythology, is a Titan, the son of Uranus (Sky) and Gaia (Earth). His name is often associated with inquisitive intellect and questioning, symbolizing the celestial axis around which the heavens revolve. As such, Coeus represents the pillar of the north, a fundamental aspect of the cosmic architecture in ancient Greek cosmology. His role in mythology, like many of the Titans, is more foundational and symbolic than active in terms of narratives or adventures.

Coeus married his sister Phoebe, another Titaness, and together they had two daughters, Leto and Asteria. Through his offspring, Coeus's influence extends into the more familiar Olympian myths. Leto becomes significant as the mother of Apollo and Artemis, two important Olympian gods. Asteria, meanwhile, is associated with the stars and prophetic dreams.

Coeus's legacy in Greek mythology is primarily through his descendants. Apollo, in particular, inherits aspects of Coeus's domain, notably in prophecy and knowledge. The Oracle of Delphi, which was initially dedicated to Gaia and later to Phoebe, eventually came under the auspices of Apollo, thus continuing Coeus's lineage in the realm of knowledge and prophecy. In the Titanomachy, the war between the Titans and the Olympians, Coeus, like his Titan brethren, was defeated and banished to Tartarus. Despite his relatively minor role in Greek mythology, Coeus's association with intellectual inquiry and the celestial order underscores the Greek reverence for knowledge and the cosmos.

Phoebe

Phoebe, in Greek mythology, is a Titaness, a daughter of the primordial deities Uranus (Sky) and Gaia (Earth). Her name, meaning "bright" or "radiant," aligns with her association as a goddess of intellect and prophecy. Phoebe is often regarded as a deity of the "bright" intellect, embodying the aspects of prophetic wisdom and luminous thought, which are crucial in the ancient Greek reverence for knowledge and foresight.

Phoebe married her brother Coeus, another Titan, and together they had two daughters, Leto and Asteria. Through her children and later her grandchildren, Apollo and Artemis (children of Leto), Phoebe's influence extends into the more prominent narratives of Greek mythology. She is especially connected to the Oracle of Delphi, initially dedicated to Gaia and later associated with Apollo, her grandson. This association underscores her role in the realm of prophecy and oracular knowledge.

While Phoebe does not feature prominently in mythological tales as an active character, her presence is significant in the divine lineage. As a Titaness, her role is more symbolic and foundational, representing the passage of divine traits and roles from the older generation of Titans to the newer Olympian gods. Phoebe's legacy lies in her embodiment of bright, clear intellect and her contribution to the lineage of prophecy and divine wisdom in Greek mythology. Her importance in the cosmic order of Greek mythos is reflective of the value placed on wisdom and forethought in ancient Greek culture.

Iapetus

Iapetus is a significant figure in Greek mythology, known as one of the Titans, the children of the primordial deities Uranus (Sky) and Gaia (Earth). His name is often associated with the meaning "the Piercer," which can be linked to his role as a Titan of mortality and craftsmanship. Iapetus represents a more obscure aspect of the Greek mythological pantheon, focusing less on cosmic or elemental powers and more on the human condition, specifically mortality and the passing of time.

Iapetus's most notable contribution to Greek mythology comes through his offspring. He married Clymene, an Oceanid, and fathered several important figures, including Atlas, who bore the sky on his shoulders; Prometheus, the benefactor of mankind known for stealing fire from the gods and giving it to humans; Epimetheus, associated with afterthought and the creation of animals; and Menoetius, a symbol of violent anger and rash action. These children play significant roles in various myths, especially Prometheus, whose stories are among the most celebrated in Greek mythology.

Despite his background role in the myths, Iapetus's lineage is crucial in shaping many key mythological narratives. Through Prometheus and Epimetheus, he is linked to the creation and the plight of humanity, bringing in themes of foresight, creativity, and the consequences of defiance against the gods. Iapetus himself, like many of the Titans, is overthrown by the Olympian gods during the Titanomachy and is subsequently confined to Tartarus, the deep abyss used for imprisoning defeated deities. Iapetus's story, therefore, represents the transition of power from the old generation of deities to the new Olympian order, as well as the complexities and vulnerabilities inherent in the human condition, as reflected through his descendants.

Themis

Themis, in Greek mythology, is a Titaness, the daughter of the primordial deities Uranus (Sky) and Gaia (Earth). Her name is intrinsically linked to the concept of divine law and order, and she personifies the natural and moral order of things. Themis represents the law as it is applied by customs and communities, embodying principles of justice, fairness, and good governance that were central to Greek society.

As a deity, Themis holds a crucial place in the pantheon of Greek gods. She was an advisor and consort to Zeus, emphasizing her role as a figure of wisdom and counsel in the divine realm. Themis is credited with bringing the Oracle of Delphi to the world, one of the most important oracular sites in ancient Greece. She also presided over the proper conduct of assembly, hospitality, and oaths, which were fundamental components of social and political life in ancient Greece.

Themis's role extends beyond her advisory duties to Zeus; she is also the mother of various significant offspring, including the Horae (goddesses of the seasons) and the Moirai (also known as the Fates), who controlled the destiny of mortals. These children further symbolize her connection to the natural order and the inescapable fate of all beings.

In art and literature, Themis is often depicted as a stern yet benevolent figure, holding a pair of scales or a cornucopia, symbols of justice and abundance. Her legacy in Greek mythology is her embodiment of the divine law and order, playing a pivotal role in maintaining the balance and structure of both the cosmic order and the societal norms of the ancient Greeks. Themis's presence in the mythos underscores the importance of law, fairness, and moral integrity in the ancient world.

Mnemosyne

Mnemosyne, in Greek mythology, is a Titaness, the daughter of the primordial deities Uranus (Sky) and Gaia (Earth). Her name directly translates to "memory," and she personifies this crucial aspect of human consciousness and experience. Mnemosyne represents the power and significance of memory, not just in terms of personal recollection but also in the broader context of the collective memory and history of peoples and cultures.

Mnemosyne's most significant role in mythology is her union with Zeus, from which the nine Muses were born. Each of these Muses presides over a different realm of the arts and sciences, symbolizing the various ways in which memory and knowledge are preserved and celebrated in culture. These daughters include Calliope (epic poetry), Clio (history), Erato (love poetry), Euterpe (music), Melpomene (tragedy), Polyhymnia (sacred poetry), Terpsichore (dance), Thalia (comedy), and Urania (astronomy).

Aside from being the mother of the Muses, Mnemosyne is also associated with a pool in Hades, opposite the river Lethe. Souls of the dead drank from Lethe so they would forget their past lives, but initiates were encouraged to drink from Mnemosyne's pool, which allowed them to remember.

In the Greek cultural context, Mnemosyne's role is profound. She is not merely a figure of rote memorization but represents the deeper significance of remembrance as a link to tradition, culture, and identity. Her presence in Greek mythology highlights the respect and importance the Greeks placed on the preservation of knowledge, history, and the arts, and she serves as a divine symbol of the continuity and legacy of human civilization.

Crius

Crius, in Greek mythology, is one of the Titans, a son of Uranus (Sky) and Gaia (Earth). Among the Titans, Crius is somewhat less prominent, with his role and attributes not as clearly defined as some of his siblings. His name is sometimes interpreted to mean 'ram' or linked to the concept of a celestial body, such as a constellation.

Crius's primary significance in mythology arises from his offspring. He married his half-sister Eurybia, a daughter of Gaia and Pontus (the Sea), and they had several children who played more notable roles in the Greek mythological canon. These children include Astraeus (the Titan god of the dusk and the winds), Pallas (a Titan associated with war), and Perses (the Titan god of destruction and peace). Through Astraeus, Crius is the grandfather of the Anemoi (the Winds) and the Astra Planeta (the Wandering Stars or Planets), including notable figures like Eosphorus (the Morning Star).

Crius's legacy in mythology is thus more through his descendants than his own direct actions. His lineage contributes significantly to various aspects of the natural world, such as the winds and stars, which were of immense importance to the ancient Greeks in terms of navigation, agriculture, and astrology. Crius, like many of his fellow Titans, was eventually overthrown by the Olympian gods during the Titanomachy and was imprisoned in Tartarus. His role in the Greek mythological landscape, while not as active or vivid as some other deities, represents the foundational and generative aspects of the Titan generation, contributing to the broader tapestry of Greek cosmology and the natural world.

In addition to these primary Titans, there were second-generation Titans, born from the first generation. Notable among these are the children of Iapetus—Prometheus, Epimetheus, Atlas, and Menoetius—and the children of Hyperion—Helios, Selene, and Eos. The term "Titan" is sometimes broadly used to include these second-generation Titans as well.

Chapter 2: The Olympians

The Olympian gods in Greek mythology are a group of deities who were believed to reside on Mount Olympus. Each god had a distinct personality, domain, and story associated with them. In this chapter, we will introduce you to these fascinating deities.

Zeus

Zeus is the most prominent and powerful figure in Greek mythology, revered as the king of the gods and the ruler of Mount Olympus. His domain encompasses the sky, thunder, lightning, law, order, and justice. Zeus is the son of the Titans Cronus and Rhea, and his story is central to the narrative of the Greek mythological cosmos.

The tale of Zeus's rise to power is one of the most well-known myths. His father, Cronus, fearing that he would be overthrown by his offspring just as he had overthrown his own father Uranus, swallowed each of his children at birth. Rhea, distressed by the loss of her children, tricked Cronus by hiding Zeus at birth and giving Cronus a stone wrapped in swaddling clothes to swallow instead. Zeus was raised in secrecy, and when he came of age, he led a rebellion against Cronus and the Titans, resulting in the Titanomachy, a cataclysmic war. After their victory, Zeus and his siblings (Hestia, Hera, Poseidon, Demeter, and Hades) divided the cosmos amongst themselves, with Zeus claiming the heavens as his domain.

As the supreme deity, Zeus played a central role in many Greek myths and was often depicted as a powerful, regal figure, wielding a thunderbolt, his most iconic symbol. Despite being the upholder of law and order, Zeus was also known for his numerous liaisons with goddesses, nymphs, and mortal women, resulting in a vast number of offspring, including many heroes and other significant figures in Greek mythology. These stories often highlight the complexities of his character, blending his kingly and judicial aspects with his more human, fallible traits.

Zeus's influence extended beyond mythology into the religious practices of the ancient Greeks. He was worshipped across the Greek world, with major temples like the one at Olympia, where the Olympic Games were held in his honor. In Greek culture and thought, Zeus represented the ultimate authority, the arbiter of justice and the enforcer of divine and moral law, embodying the Greeks' understanding of cosmic order and the human condition.

Hera

Hera is a central figure in Greek mythology, known as the queen of the gods and the wife and sister of Zeus. She is the daughter of the Titans Cronus and Rhea, and her domain includes marriage, women, childbirth, and family. Hera is one of the most important and powerful goddesses in the Greek pantheon, embodying the ideals of matrimony and the sanctity of the family unit.

Hera's marriage to Zeus was not without its problems, primarily due to Zeus's numerous infidelities. Much of Hera's mythological narrative involves her reactions to Zeus's extramarital affairs and the children born from them. Despite these challenges, Hera maintained her status and power as the queen of the gods. She is often depicted as a majestic and solemn figure, embodying both the dignity and the wrath associated with her role as the goddess of marriage and fidelity.

In mythology, Hera's character is complex. While she is venerated as a protector of women and presider over marital harmony, she is also known for her jealousy and vengeful nature, particularly towards Zeus's lovers and their offspring. Among her notable acts of vengeance include the trials imposed upon Heracles, Zeus's son by a mortal woman.

Hera's worship was widespread in ancient Greece, and she was honored with numerous temples and festivals, such as the Heraia. In art and literature, she is often portrayed as a regal, imposing figure, sometimes holding a pomegranate, a symbol of fertility. Hera's role in Greek mythology highlights the ancient Greeks' views on the sanctity and complexities of marriage and family, and her figure represents both the nurturing aspects and the challenges inherent in these institutions.

Poseidon

Poseidon is a major deity in Greek mythology, known as the god of the sea, earthquakes, storms, and horses. He is one of the twelve Olympian gods and the brother of Zeus and Hades. Poseidon is the son of the Titans Cronus and Rhea, and like his siblings, he played a significant role in overthrowing the Titans and establishing the rule of the Olympians.

As the god of the sea, Poseidon holds sway over all bodies of water, and by extension, is a patron of sailors and fishermen. He is often depicted carrying his trident, a three-pronged spear, with which he could stir the waters, create storms, and even cause earthquakes – a phenomenon frequently experienced in Greece and attributed to his wrath or interventions. Poseidon's temperament was considered as turbulent as the sea, capable of being calm and benevolent but also tempestuous and destructive.

Poseidon also had a significant role in the mythological stories of numerous Greek heroes and was involved in various disputes with other gods. One of the most famous of these is his contest with Athena over the patronage of the city of Athens, which Athena won. Additionally, Poseidon was revered as the creator of horses, and his connection to these animals is a recurrent theme in myths and iconography.

Poseidon's influence extends to various aspects of ancient Greek life. He was widely worshipped, especially in coastal cities and towns, and many temples and shrines were dedicated to him. In Greek art, he is typically represented as a robust, mature man with a dense beard, often riding a chariot pulled by hippocamps (sea horses). His domain over the sea, a crucial element for the Greeks, who were skilled sailors and navigators, underscores his importance in Greek mythology and culture, embodying the power, unpredictability, and essential nature of the sea in the ancient Greek worldview.

Demeter

Demeter is a prominent goddess, revered as the deity of agriculture, harvest, fertility, and sacred law. She is one of the twelve Olympian gods and is the daughter of the Titans Cronus and Rhea, making her a sister to Zeus, Hera, Hades, Poseidon, and Hestia. Demeter's role in the Greek pantheon is crucial, as she governs the growth and productivity of crops, and by extension, the cycle of life and death in nature.

The most famous myth involving Demeter is the story of her daughter Persephone's abduction by Hades, the god of the underworld. Grief-stricken by her daughter's disappearance, Demeter withdrew her gifts from the world, causing a great famine as the earth became barren. This myth explains the seasons: when Persephone is in the underworld, Demeter mourns and winter ensues; her joy upon Persephone's return in the spring causes the earth to bloom. This cycle symbolizes the ancient Greek understanding of agricultural cycles and the natural rhythms of growth and decay.

Demeter is also central to the Eleusinian Mysteries, ancient religious rites held in her honor, which promised initiates guidance for a blessed afterlife. These mysteries were among the most sacred and significant religious rituals in ancient Greece and highlight Demeter's role as a bridge between the living and the dead, and between the divine and the human realms.

In art, Demeter is often depicted as a mature, matronly figure, usually holding sheaves of wheat or a cornucopia, symbols of abundance. Her character embodies the nurturing aspect of the earth, the importance of agriculture in sustaining life, and the deep connection between the divine and the natural world. Demeter's myths and worship reflect the ancient Greeks' reverence for the earth's fertility and their understanding of the intricate balances within the natural world.

Athena

Athena, in Greek mythology, is one of the most revered Olympian gods, known as the goddess of wisdom, handicraft, and warfare. She is a daughter of Zeus, born in a unique manner: she sprang fully grown and armed from Zeus's head, a symbol of her role as a deity of intellect and strategic warfare. Unlike Ares, the god of war who represents the brutal, chaotic aspect of battle, Athena embodies the strategic and just side of warfare, as well as wisdom and skill in crafts.

Athena is most famously known for her role in various Greek heroic tales. She is the patron goddess of the city of Athens, which was named in her honor after she gifted the olive tree to the Athenians in a contest with Poseidon. Athena also played a crucial role in the story of Odysseus, guiding and aiding him throughout his journey home in Homer's "Odyssey." Her involvement with heroes like Perseus and Heracles further underscores her role as a protector and supporter of heroes and their endeavors.

In addition to her martial aspects, Athena is associated with wisdom, reason, and intelligence. She is often depicted with an owl, symbolizing wisdom, and wearing a helmet and carrying a shield, representing her warrior aspect. Athena's virginity is also a significant element of her mythology, indicating her independence and symbolizing her role as a parthenos, a maiden untied to a husband or traditional domestic roles.

Athena's temples and festivals, notably the Panathenaia in Athens, were central to Greek religious and civic life. Her influence in Greek culture and mythology is profound, representing the ancient Greek ideals of wisdom, strategic warfare, and skill. Athena's character, blending intelligence with martial prowess and crafts, embodies the Greek respect for knowledge, strategy, and the arts, making her one of the most complex and revered deities in the Greek pantheon.

Apollo

Apollo is a major deity in Greek mythology, renowned as the god of the sun, light, music, poetry, healing, and prophecy. He is the son of Zeus and Leto, and the twin brother of Artemis, the goddess of the hunt and moon. Born on the island of Delos, Apollo quickly rose to prominence among the Olympian gods, embodying a wide range of ideal attributes and cultural values.

Apollo is often depicted as the epitome of youthful beauty and athleticism, representing the ideal of kouros, a beardless, athletic youth. He is associated with the sun and light, driving his chariot across the sky to bring daylight to the earth. This aspect of his mythology highlights the importance of the sun in the ancient Greek world – as a source of life, light, and order.

Aside from his solar attributes, Apollo is also revered as the god of music and the arts, often depicted with a lyre, which he played masterfully. He led the Muses, the goddesses of artistic inspiration, and was considered the patron of music, poetry, and the arts. His oracular shrine at Delphi, where he communicated through the Pythia or the Oracle of Delphi, was one of the most important in the ancient world, where people from all over came for guidance.

Apollo also had a role as a healer and a bringer of plague, showcasing his dual nature in matters of health and disease. His myths are numerous and varied, including his tragic love affairs, his vengeful nature when wronged, and his guidance of heroes.

In Greek culture and religion, Apollo occupied a central place, with numerous temples and festivals dedicated to him. He symbolized order, harmony, and balance, contrasting with the wild and untamed aspects of nature often represented by his twin sister, Artemis. Apollo's multifaceted role in Greek mythology reflects the ancient Greeks' admiration for beauty, art, music, reason, and the harmonious order of the natural world.

Artemis

Artemis is a key figure in Greek mythology, renowned as the goddess of the hunt, wilderness, moon, and archery. She is the daughter of Zeus and Leto and the twin sister of Apollo, the god of the sun. Artemis is often depicted as a huntress carrying a bow and arrows, and she is associated with wild animals and forests, symbolizing the untamed and primal aspects of nature.

Artemis was born on the island of Ortygia, with some myths stating that she helped her mother, Leto, give birth to her twin brother Apollo, immediately after her own birth. This story highlights her association with childbirth and the protection of young life, despite being a virgin goddess herself. Artemis's virginity is a significant aspect of her mythology, symbolizing her independence, autonomy, and alignment with the natural world, free from the constraints of traditional marital and domestic roles.

As the goddess of the hunt, Artemis is often shown in the company of nymphs and wild animals, roaming the forests and mountains. She is revered as a protector of the young and a guardian of the wilderness. Her Roman equivalent, Diana, shares similar attributes.

Artemis's character in mythology is complex and multifaceted. She is seen as both a nurturer and a fierce protector, quick to defend her independence and purity, as well as those of her followers. Famous myths involving Artemis include the transformation of the hunter Actaeon into a stag and the tale of Orion, a giant and hunter who gained her favor but was later killed.

Artemis was widely worshipped across the Greek world, with numerous temples and sacred groves dedicated to her. Her festivals often involved themes of transition from childhood to adulthood, reflecting her role as a protector of the young. Artemis's mythology embodies the wild, untamed aspects of nature and the concept of chastity and independence, making her a powerful and revered figure in the ancient Greek pantheon.

Ares

Ares is the god of war, representing the brutal and violent aspects of battle. He is one of the twelve Olympian gods, the son of Zeus and Hera. Unlike his sister Athena, who symbolizes strategic warfare and wisdom in battle, Ares embodies the chaotic, destructive, and bloodthirsty side of war.

Ares's character in Greek mythology is complex and often negative. He is depicted as fierce and aggressive, reveling in the tumult and havoc of combat without regard for justice or righteousness. This portrayal contrasts with the more honorable and valorous view of warfare represented by other cultures, reflecting the ancient Greeks' ambivalence about the horrors of war and its consequences. Despite being a god, Ares is not invincible and is sometimes depicted as being on the losing side of conflicts, even wounded in battle.

Ares's relationships with other gods and mortals in Greek myths often highlight his aggressive nature. His affair with Aphrodite, the goddess of love, and the resulting narrative threads, including the birth of several children like Eros and Harmonia, create a compelling contrast between love and war. His involvement in the Trojan War, where he sided with the Trojans, is a notable episode in his mythology.

In terms of worship, Ares's cult was not as extensive or as widespread as that of other Olympian gods. He was revered more in Sparta, the Greek city-state known for its military prowess, where he symbolized the ideals of Spartan warfare. In art, Ares is often depicted as a fully armed warrior, young and powerful, embodying the physical vigor and relentless nature of war. While not the most favored among the gods, Ares's role in Greek mythology is significant, representing the intrinsic and inescapable aspects of conflict and violence in human society.

Aphrodite

Aphrodite is a prominent figure in Greek mythology, celebrated as the goddess of love, beauty, and sexuality. According to the most famous myth of her origin, she was born from the foam of the sea, arising near the island of Cyprus. This birth story gives her the epithet "foam-born" or "Aphros." In another version, she is described as the daughter of Zeus and Dione, an early Greek goddess.

Aphrodite's role in Greek myths is often associated with love and romantic desire, but she also embodies the generative powers of nature and the life-giving forces of the earth. Her influence is seen in the numerous love affairs and liaisons she had with both gods and mortals, leading to the birth of several other important deities and heroes, including Eros (Cupid), Aeneas, and Harmonia. Her most famous mortal lover was Adonis.

One of the most well-known myths involving Aphrodite is her role in the Judgment of Paris, which indirectly led to the Trojan War. Paris, a prince of Troy, chose Aphrodite as the fairest goddess over Hera and Athena, after she promised him the most beautiful woman in the world, Helen of Sparta. This decision ultimately led to the outbreak of the Trojan War.

Aphrodite's worship was widespread throughout the Greek world, with numerous temples and festivals dedicated to her. She was often portrayed as a figure of irresistible beauty and charm, capable of enthralling both gods and men. In art, she was frequently depicted as a stunningly beautiful, sensuous woman, embodying the ideals of Greek beauty and femininity.

Her character in mythology, while centered around themes of love and attraction, also encompasses aspects of jealousy, rivalry, and the complexities of relationships, both divine and mortal. Aphrodite's influence extends beyond mere physical attraction, symbolizing the creative and destructive powers of love and desire in the human experience. Her presence in Greek mythology and culture reflects the ancient Greeks' understanding of the powerful and often uncontrollable forces of love and beauty.

Hephaestus

Hephaestus, in Greek mythology, is the god of fire, metalworking, stone masonry, forges, and the art of sculpture. He is known for his skillful craftsmanship and is revered as the blacksmith of the gods, creating their weapons and armor. He is the son of Zeus and Hera, although in some myths, he is said to have been born from Hera alone, without a father. Hephaestus is often depicted as a bearded man holding a hammer and anvil, the tools of a blacksmith, and is notable for being the only Olympian god with a physical disability – he is lame in both legs.

One of the most significant myths about Hephaestus concerns his birth. He was cast out of Olympus by his mother Hera because of his deformity, or in another version, by Zeus for intervening in a quarrel between Zeus and Hera. He fell into the sea and was rescued by sea nymphs who raised him. This fall and subsequent resentment towards his parents, particularly Hera, are crucial elements of his mythology.

Hephaestus's role in Greek myths often revolves around his incredible skill as a craftsman. He created many of the gods' wondrous artifacts, including Zeus's thunderbolt, the armor of Achilles, and the girdle of Aphrodite. He also fashioned the first woman, Pandora, on Zeus's orders. His own armor and palace on Olympus are said to be marvels of artisanship.

Despite his physical imperfections and often being the subject of mockery, Hephaestus is depicted as a peace-loving, kind, and benevolent god. His marriage to Aphrodite, the goddess of love and beauty, is another central narrative, often highlighting the contrast between his grotesque appearance and her beauty, and her numerous affairs.

In the cultural and religious life of ancient Greece, Hephaestus was highly revered, especially in industrial and manufacturing centers. Festivals celebrating his craft were common, and his temples were places of artisanship and creativity. Hephaestus symbolizes the mastery over fire, the transformative power of creativity, and the respect for skilled craft and labor in Greek society. His myths serve as a reminder of the value of resilience, ingenuity, and the ability to overcome adversity.

Hermes

Hermes is a significant deity in Greek mythology, renowned for his versatility, cunning, and as a messenger of the gods. He is the son of Zeus and the Pleiad Maia, born in a cave on Mount Cyllene in Arcadia. Hermes is one of the twelve Olympian gods and is depicted as a youthful, athletic figure, often wearing winged sandals (talaria) and a winged hat (petasos), and carrying a herald's staff known as a caduceus.

Hermes's role in Greek mythology is multifaceted. He is the god of trade, commerce, and the market, as well as of thieves, travelers, sports, athletes, and border crossings. He serves as a guide to the Underworld, leading souls to the afterlife, and as a messenger, he is the communicator between the gods and mortals, known for his speed and eloquence. This association with various aspects of life reflects his character as a cunning, resourceful, and adaptable deity.

One of the most famous myths about Hermes is his theft of Apollo's cattle on the day he was born, showcasing his cleverness and ingenuity. In reparation for this theft, he crafted the lyre and gave it to Apollo, establishing a lifelong bond between them. Hermes also played a crucial role in many Greek myths and epics, including serving as Odysseus's ally in Homer's "Odyssey" and as a helper to Perseus and Heracles in their adventures.

In addition to his mythological role, Hermes was widely worshipped throughout the Greek world. He was revered as the protector of travelers and shepherds, and herms, stone pillars with his head and phallus, were often placed at crossroads and boundaries as a form of protection. Hermes's symbolism in Greek culture is vast, representing communication, commerce, cunning, and transition – from the material world to the afterlife, from youth to adulthood, and across physical and metaphorical boundaries. His character embodies the Greek ideals of wit, agility, and adaptability, making him a beloved and enduring figure in Greek mythology and culture.

Dionysus

Dionysus, in Greek mythology, is a unique and complex deity known as the god of wine, parties, festivals, madness, chaos, drunkenness, vegetation, and ecstasy. He is the son of Zeus and the mortal princess Semele, making him the only Olympian god with a mortal mother. His birth story is extraordinary: Semele perished due to the sight of Zeus in his true form, and Zeus saved the unborn Dionysus by sewing him into his thigh until he was ready to be born. This unusual birth contributes to Dionysus's dual nature as both divine and mortal.

Dionysus is often depicted as an outsider god, bringing a cult of ecstasy and madness that was contrary to the ordered, civilized culture of the Greeks. His followers, including the Maenads (wild women) and Satyrs (half-man, half-goat creatures), engaged in frenzied dances and revelries, symbolizing the liberating and irrational aspects of his nature. These rituals were central to the worship of Dionysus, reflecting his power to transcend the ordinary limits of human experience, blurring the boundaries between the civilized and the primal.

Dionysus's mythology is rich with themes of death and rebirth, reflecting the perennial cycle of nature's growth and decay, akin to the process of winemaking. He is a god of contradictions: both joyous and terrifying, youthful and yet an old man, born of fire and nursed by rain. His most famous myth involves his descent into Hades to retrieve his mother Semele, whom he then brings to Olympus.

In ancient Greek society, Dionysus was a highly significant deity. His festivals, the Dionysia and the Bacchanalia, were important religious events, known for their theatrical competitions that laid the foundation for Greek tragedy and comedy. In art, Dionysus is often depicted as a beardless, sensuous, effeminate youth, or sometimes as a mature man with a beard, holding a wine cup (kantharos) and a thyrsus (a staff entwined with ivy and topped with a pinecone). His character embodies the concept of divine ecstasy and uninhibited joy, but also the inherent dangers of excess, making him a multifaceted symbol of human experience in Greek mythology and culture.

Two Additional Gods

In Greek mythology, two other deities are sometimes included among the Olympian gods, expanding the usual twelve to fourteen. These are Hestia and Hades.

Hestia

Hestia, in Greek mythology, is a revered and important deity, known as the goddess of the hearth, home, and domesticity. She is one of the twelve Olympian gods, the firstborn child of the Titans Cronus and Rhea, making her a sibling to gods such as Zeus, Hera, Poseidon, Demeter, and Hades. However, in later traditions she is replaced in the Olympians by Dionysus. Unlike many of her more flamboyant siblings, Hestia is characterized by her gentle, non-confrontational nature.

Hestia's role in Greek mythology and religion is unique. She does not have a series of adventures or conquests like other gods, but her presence is integral to the stability and sanctity of the home and family. She is the embodiment of the household fire and is honored in every home and at public hearths. In every city, her sacred fire burned continuously, symbolizing the unity and stability of the community. If a new colony was to be founded, flames from Hestia's hearth in the mother city would be carried to the new settlement, signifying continuity and kinship.

Despite her significance, Hestia is one of the least personified of the Olympian deities in art and literature. She is often depicted as a modestly veiled woman, sometimes holding a flowering branch. There are few, if any, myths that tell of her personal endeavors or relationships. Hestia famously chose to remain an eternal virgin, refusing the marriage proposals of Poseidon and Apollo, and thus she is also a symbol of personal autonomy and integrity.

In the religious practices of ancient Greece, Hestia's cult was not characterized by spectacular rituals or festivals but was marked by the simple daily offerings at the household hearth. Her gentle character and the centrality of her domain in everyday life made her an omnipresent and much-beloved figure in Greek mythology, representing the warmth and sacredness of the home. Her presence in

Greek religion underscores the importance of the hearth and home as the center of family and community life.

Hades

Hades, in Greek mythology, is the god of the underworld and the ruler of the dead. He is one of the Olympian gods, though he resides not on Mount Olympus but in his dark realm beneath the earth. Hades is the eldest son of the Titans Cronus and Rhea, making him the brother of Zeus, Hera, Poseidon, Demeter, and Hestia.

After the overthrow of the Titans, the world was divided among the three brothers, Zeus, Poseidon, and Hades, through a draw. Hades drew the underworld, becoming its ruler, while Zeus ruled the sky, and Poseidon the sea. Hades' kingdom is often described as a shadowy, dismal place, but it is also a place of final justice, where souls are judged after death. The underworld, also known as Hades, is divided into various regions, including the Elysian Fields, the Asphodel Meadows, and Tartarus.

Hades is often portrayed as a stern, unyielding figure, embodying the inevitability of death. Despite his fearsome reputation, Hades is not evil; he is more of a just ruler, maintaining balance and order in the afterlife. He is rarely depicted leaving his underworld kingdom, and his interactions with the other gods and the mortal world are limited.

One of the most famous myths involving Hades is the abduction of Persephone, daughter of Demeter, whom he took to be his queen in the underworld. This act led to the creation of the seasons, according to Greek myth, as Demeter, in her grief, caused the earth to become barren when Persephone was with Hades, resulting in winter, and allowed things to grow again when she returned to the surface, bringing spring and summer.

In Greek religious practice, Hades was respected but not widely worshipped. His name was often avoided in speech, leading to euphemisms such as "the Rich One" or "the Hospitable One." In art, he is often depicted as a regal, bearded figure, holding a scepter or a key, symbolizing his control over the underworld. Hades' role in Greek mythology is essential, representing the natural cycle of life and death and the notion of an afterlife where the soul faces the consequences of its earthly life.

Chapter 3: Other Characters

G reek mythology is rich with a wide array of characters that don't fall into the category of gods, ranging from demigods and heroes to monsters, creatures, and notable mortals. In this chapter, we will introduce you to many of these interesting characters that play roles in the Greek myths.

Heracles

Heracles, known as Hercules in Roman mythology, is one of the most celebrated and renowned heroes in Greek mythology. He is the son of Zeus and Alcmene, a mortal woman, making him a demigod. Born with extraordinary strength, Heracles is best known for his incredible feats and adventures, most notably the Twelve Labors, a series of tasks he performed as penance for a crime.

The story of Heracles begins with his miraculous birth, marked by Zeus's desire to have an offspring who would be a hero among men. Hera, Zeus's wife, out of jealousy, tried to hinder Heracles's birth and later inflicted him with madness, causing him to commit a grave act. As atonement, Heracles was required to perform the Twelve Labors, tasks so difficult and dangerous they seemed impossible. These labors included slaying the Nemean Lion, capturing the Golden Hind of Artemis, obtaining the Girdle of Hippolyta, Queen of the Amazons, capturing the Erymanthian Boar, cleaning the Augean stables in a single day, and obtaining the Cattle of Geryon.

Apart from the Labors, Heracles participated in numerous other adventures, demonstrating his strength, bravery, and cleverness. He aided the gods in the battle against the Giants (the Gigantomachy), joined the quest for the Golden Fleece as one of the Argonauts, and even aided the gods in their battle against the Titans.

Despite his heroic deeds, Heracles's life was fraught with challenges and tragedies, often as a result of Hera's animosity. He was known for his quick temper, but also for his sense of humor and great wisdom. After his mortal death, he was granted immortality and a place among the gods on Mount Olympus, a rare honor for a mortal.

Heracles's legacy in Greek culture is profound. He was venerated as both a hero and a god, with numerous temples dedicated to him. In art, he is often depicted as a powerful, muscular man wearing a lion's skin and wielding a club. His figure represents the ideal of the Greek hero: unparalleled strength, courage in the face of overwhelming odds, and enduring legacy in mythology and popular imagination.

Achilles

Achilles is a legendary figure in Greek mythology, renowned for his prowess as a warrior in the Trojan War. He is a central character in Homer's epic poem, the "Iliad." Achilles was the son of Peleus, the king of the Myrmidons in Thessaly, and the sea nymph Thetis. His story is one of heroism, pride, and ultimately tragedy, making him one of the most memorable figures in Greek myth and literature.

The most famous story about Achilles concerns his near invulnerability. When he was a baby, Thetis dipped him in the River Styx to make him immortal. However, she held him by his heel, which remained vulnerable – a detail that led to the phrase "Achilles' heel," signifying a critical weakness. As a warrior, Achilles was unrivaled in skill, strength, and prowess, feared by enemies and admired by allies.

Achilles's central role in the Trojan War, as depicted in the "Iliad," is marked by both his incredible feats on the battlefield and his volatile emotions. His conflict with Agamemnon, the Greek leader, over a dispute about war spoils, leads him to withdraw from battle, a crucial turn in the war. It is only after the death of his close friend and possible lover, Patroclus, at the hands of the Trojan prince Hector, that Achilles returns to combat, fueled by a desire for revenge. His killing of Hector outside the walls of Troy is one of the most famous episodes of the war.

Achilles' eventual death, as prophesized, comes from an arrow shot by the Trojan prince Paris, guided by Apollo, which strikes his vulnerable heel. His death symbolizes the tragic fall of a great hero, marked by a mixture of pride, loyalty, and unstoppable rage.

Achilles is remembered as the quintessential Greek hero, embodying the ideals of martial prowess and honor. His story, with its themes of glory, wrath, and fate, has had a lasting impact on Western culture, symbolizing the complex nature of heroism and the human condition. His character in the "Iliad" is a rich exploration of the warrior ethos in ancient Greece, as well as the costs and consequences of war.

Theseus

Theseus is a celebrated hero in Greek mythology, known for his intelligence, strength, and a series of daring adventures. He is often considered one of the greatest heroes of Greek myth, alongside figures like Heracles and Perseus. Theseus was the son of Aethra, a mortal woman, and Aegeus, the king of Athens, though some myths also claim he was the son of Poseidon, the god of the sea.

One of the most famous stories of Theseus is his journey to Athens. As a young man, he chose to take the dangerous land route to the city, during which he encountered and defeated a number of bandits and monsters, including the notorious Procrustes and Sinis. These feats established his reputation as a powerful warrior and a protector of the innocent.

The most celebrated of Theseus's adventures is his venture into the Labyrinth to slay the Minotaur, a monstrous half-man, half-bull creature. The Minotaur was kept in the Labyrinth in Crete, and every year, Athens was forced to send seven young men and seven young women as tribute to be devoured by the beast. Theseus volunteered to be one of the tributes, intent on killing the Minotaur. With the help of Ariadne, the daughter of King Minos of Crete, who gave him a ball of thread to trace his path in the Labyrinth, Theseus succeeded in his mission, a symbol of triumph over seemingly impossible challenges.

Theseus's other exploits include his journey to the Underworld with his friend Pirithous and his various romantic adventures, which often ended tragically. As a king of Athens, he was considered a wise and fair ruler who brought political and social reforms, including the synoikismos, the political unification of Attica under Athens.

Theseus's character in Greek mythology embodies the qualities of courage, justice, and intelligence. He is seen as a symbol of Athenian political and cultural supremacy, embodying the ideal Athenian hero. His adventures and accomplishments made him a beloved figure in Greek folklore, and his story has been told and retold throughout the centuries, highlighting the timeless appeal of heroic tales and the human struggle against adversity.

Perseus

Perseus is a prominent hero in Greek mythology, celebrated for his courage and various heroic feats. He is best known for beheading Medusa, one of the three Gorgon sisters with serpentine hair whose gaze could turn people to stone. Perseus was the son of Zeus and Danaë, the daughter of King Acrisius of Argos. His birth itself was miraculous, as Danaë was locked away in a bronze chamber by her father, who feared a prophecy that her son would one day kill him. Zeus, however, came to her in the form of golden rain, and Perseus was conceived.

One of Perseus's most renowned adventures is his quest to kill Medusa. King Polydectes of Seriphos, desiring Danaë, tricked Perseus into promising to bring him Medusa's head, thinking the task would be impossible and fatal. With the help of Athena and Hermes, Perseus received special equipment for his mission: winged sandals to fly, a helmet of invisibility from Hades, a reflective shield, and a sharp sword. Using the shield to view Medusa's reflection, Perseus successfully beheaded her without turning to stone. On his journey back, he had many other adventures, including rescuing and marrying Andromeda, who was to be sacrificed to a sea monster.

Perseus's life was marked by several other significant events. He accidentally fulfilled the prophecy of killing his grandfather, Acrisius, thus showing the inescapability of fate in Greek mythology. After his death, Perseus was immortalized in the stars as the constellation Perseus, alongside Andromeda and other figures from his adventures.

In Greek culture, Perseus's story was a popular subject in art and literature. He is often depicted as a brave and resourceful hero, embodying the ideal qualities of Greek heroism. His journey represents a rite of passage, symbolizing the triumph of intelligence and bravery over monstrous challenges. Perseus's tale, like those of other Greek heroes, captures the essence of the human struggle against adversity and the pursuit of noble goals.

Jason

Jason is a central figure in Greek mythology, famous as the leader of the Argonauts in the quest for the Golden Fleece. He is often depicted as a courageous but sometimes flawed hero, embodying the complex nature of Greek heroism. Jason was the son of Aeson, the rightful king of Iolcus, who was deposed by his half-brother Pelias. Raised by the centaur Chiron, Jason returned to Iolcus as a young man to reclaim his throne.

Pelias, clinging to power and fearing Jason's claim, set him a seemingly impossible task to prove his worthiness: to retrieve the Golden Fleece from Colchis, a distant and dangerous land. The

Golden Fleece, a symbol of authority and kingship, was guarded by a dragon in the sacred grove of Ares, the war god. To accomplish this feat, Jason assembled a crew of heroes, including Heracles, Orpheus, and the Boreads, aboard the ship Argo, thus beginning the famous voyage of the Argonauts.

Jason's journey was filled with perilous challenges and adventures. Upon reaching Colchis, he succeeded in his quest with the help of the sorceress Medea, King Aeëtes's daughter, who fell in love with him. Medea used her magic to help Jason overcome the trials set by her father, including yoking fire-breathing bulls and sowing dragon's teeth, which sprouted into an army of warriors. After obtaining the Fleece, Jason and Medea fled, with Medea using her sorcery to elude their pursuers.

Jason's return to Iolcus was marked by further trials and tribulations. His relationship with Medea, fraught with tension and betrayal, led to a tragic end, and Jason's own demise was inglorious. According to some versions, he died lonely and forlorn, a stark contrast to his heroic beginnings.

In Greek mythology, Jason's story is a tale of adventure, ambition, love, and ultimately, the human susceptibility to hubris and moral failings. His quest for the Golden Fleece is not only a classic hero's journey but also a complex narrative exploring themes of leadership, loyalty, and the consequences of one's choices. Jason's legacy in Greek culture is profound, serving as a cautionary tale about the price of ambition and the fleeting nature of glory.

Helen of Troy

Helen of Troy, renowned in Greek mythology as "the face that launched a thousand ships," is one of the most famous female figures in ancient Greek lore. She was considered the most beautiful woman in the world. Her story is central to the events of the Trojan War, one of the most significant narratives in Greek mythology.

Helen was the daughter of Zeus and Leda, the queen of Sparta, and was born from an egg, making her a half-sister to Castor and Pollux (the Dioscuri) and Clytemnestra. In some versions, she is described as the daughter of Tyndareus, Leda's husband and the king of Sparta, due to the dual paternity common in Greek mythology. Helen's beauty was renowned from a young age, leading to her abduction by Theseus, from which she was later rescued by her brothers.

Helen's most famous story is her role in sparking the Trojan War. She was married to Menelaus, the king of Sparta, but was abducted or eloped with Paris, a prince of Troy, an act that was often attributed to the will of Aphrodite. This event led to the Greeks, led by Menelaus and his brother Agamemnon, launching a massive expedition to retrieve her, resulting in the ten-year-long Trojan War.

Helen's character in mythology is complex; she is often portrayed as a passive figure whose beauty incites desire and conflict among men, yet some versions of the myth also hint at her sorrow and regret over the war caused in her name. After the fall of Troy, Helen returned to Sparta with Menelaus, where her beauty remained undimmed by time.

In Greek culture, Helen of Troy symbolizes both the power and the peril of beauty, and her story explores themes of desire, responsibility, and the devastating consequences of human actions. Her legacy has endured through the centuries, capturing the imagination of poets, artists, and writers, becoming a symbol of beauty and its ability to change the course of history.

Odysseus

Odysseus is a central figure in Greek mythology, renowned for his cunning, intelligence, and resourcefulness. He is most famous as the protagonist of Homer's epic, "The Odyssey," which narrates his long and arduous journey home following the Trojan War. Odysseus was the king of Ithaca, a small island kingdom, and was married to Penelope, with whom he had a son, Telemachus.

In the "Iliad," Homer's account of the Trojan War, Odysseus is depicted as a wise, eloquent, and cunning leader, known for his persuasive speech and strategic mind. He played a crucial role in many key moments of the war, including the creation of the strategy to use the Trojan Horse, a large wooden horse used to sneak Greek warriors into Troy, leading to the city's fall.

"The Odyssey" focuses on Odysseus's ten-year journey back to Ithaca after the end of the Trojan War. This journey was fraught with challenges and trials set by various gods and mythical creatures. Odysseus encountered the Cyclops Polyphemus, the enchantress Circe, the Sirens, and journeyed to the Underworld, among other adventures. His intelligence and adaptability were his greatest assets, helping him to overcome these obstacles.

Odysseus's character is marked by both heroism and human flaws. His longing for home and family drives many of his actions, but he also faces and succumbs to various temptations and makes decisions that prolong his journey. Upon returning to Ithaca, Odysseus finds his home overrun by suitors vying for Penelope's hand, believing Odysseus to be dead. With the help of Telemachus and Athena, Odysseus defeats the suitors and reclaims his throne and family.

In Greek mythology and culture, Odysseus represents the archetype of the clever hero, using wit and strategy rather than brute force to overcome challenges. His story is a complex exploration of themes like the longing for home, the trials of heroism, and the human struggle against both external challenges and personal weaknesses. Odysseus's legacy has profoundly influenced Western literature and storytelling, embodying the enduring human journey against adversity.

Atalanta

Atalanta is a notable character in Greek mythology, distinguished as a swift-footed huntress and a formidable warrior. She stands out in Greek myth as one of the few prominent female heroes in a predominantly male-dominated heroic tradition.

According to legend, Atalanta was the daughter of King Iasus of Arcadia, who, disappointed at having a daughter instead of a son, left her on a mountainside to die. However, a she-bear, sent by Artemis, the goddess of the hunt, nursed and cared for her. Growing up in the wilderness, Atalanta became a skilled hunter and was fiercely protective of her independence and virginity.

One of Atalanta's most famous myths is her participation in the Calydonian Boar hunt. The boar was sent by Artemis to ravage the land of Calydon as punishment for neglecting her in a sacrifice. Atalanta joined the hunt with many famous heroes, and she was the first to draw blood from the beast, eventually helping to bring it down. Her prowess in the hunt earned her respect and admiration from her male counterparts.

Another notable aspect of Atalanta's myth is her race with suitors. She agreed to marry only if a suitor could outrun her in a footrace, knowing her swift speed made defeat unlikely. Many tried and failed, losing their lives in the process, as the penalty for losing the race was death. It was Hippomenes (or Melanion, in some versions) who finally won her hand, not through speed but by cunning. With the help of Aphrodite, he used three golden apples to distract Atalanta during the race, winning both the race and her hand in marriage.

Bellerophon

Bellerophon is a hero in Greek mythology, renowned for his bravery and adventures, most notably for taming and riding the winged horse

Pegasus and slaying the Chimera, a fearsome monster with a lion's head, a goat's body, and a serpent's tail. He is often depicted as a symbol of audacious ambition, illustrating both the heights of heroic achievement and the dangers of hubris.

Bellerophon's story begins with his exile after being falsely accused of a crime. He took refuge in the court of King Proetus, whose wife, Queen Stheneboea (or Anteia), fell in love with him. When Bellerophon rejected her advances, she falsely accused him of trying to seduce her. King Proetus, unwilling to kill Bellerophon due to the laws of hospitality, sent him to King Iobates of Lycia with a sealed message requesting that Iobates kill the bearer. Recognizing Bellerophon's noble character, Iobates instead set him on a series of seemingly impossible tasks, the first of which was to slay the Chimera.

To accomplish this feat, Bellerophon needed the help of Pegasus, the divine winged horse born from the blood of Medusa. With guidance from the seer Polyeidos, Bellerophon slept in Athena's temple, where the goddess visited him in a dream, giving him a golden bridle to tame Pegasus. After successfully capturing and taming Pegasus, Bellerophon went on to complete his first task, slaying the Chimera from the air.

Bellerophon's subsequent adventures, including his battles against the Solymi and the Amazons, further established his reputation as a hero. However, his story ends in tragedy. Overcome with pride, Bellerophon attempted to ride Pegasus to Olympus to join the gods. Zeus, angered by his presumption, sent a gadfly to sting Pegasus, causing Bellerophon to fall back to Earth. He spent the rest of his life crippled and in misery, shunned by both gods and mortals.

Bellerophon's tale in Greek mythology serves as a cautionary narrative about the consequences of overreaching ambition and the importance of understanding one's place in the world. His initial successes exemplify the virtues of courage and resourcefulness, but his eventual downfall underscores the Greek concept of hubris — excessive pride or self-confidence — and its inevitable consequences.

Orpheus

Orpheus is a legendary figure in Greek mythology, renowned for his extraordinary musical talent and tragic love story. He is often depicted as one of the greatest poets and musicians of the ancient world, with a lyre that could charm all living things and even inanimate objects. Orpheus was said to be the son of Calliope, the Muse of epic poetry, and either Oeagrus, a king of Thrace, or Apollo, the god of music.

The most famous myth about Orpheus is his descent into the Underworld to retrieve his wife, Eurydice. After Eurydice died from a snake bite, Orpheus, grief-stricken, played such sorrowful songs that the gods and nymphs advised him to travel to the Underworld to bring her back. Moved by his music, Hades and Persephone, the rulers of the Underworld, agreed to let Eurydice return with him to the living world on one condition: Orpheus must not look back at her until they had reached the surface. Tragically, just before they reached the light of day, Orpheus, overcome with anxiety and love, turned to look at her, and she vanished back into the Underworld forever.

Orpheus's life after Eurydice's second death was marked by sorrow and loneliness. He wandered the earth, playing his music but forever mourning his lost love. According to various versions of the myth, his death was violent and gruesome, involving Maenads (followers of Dionysus) tearing him apart. After his death, it was said that Orpheus's head continued to sing as it floated down the river to the sea.

In Greek culture, Orpheus was revered not only as a musician but also as a poet and prophet. He was associated with the Orphic mysteries, religious rites and teachings that offered insights into the afterlife and the secrets of the universe. The story of Orpheus and Eurydice has been retold in countless forms over the centuries, resonating through Western literature and art. It is a powerful tale of love, loss, and the transformative power of art, encapsulating the profound human experiences of passion and grief.

Cerberus

Cerberus is a prominent and fearsome figure in Greek mythology, known as the guard dog of the Underworld. This monstrous creature is most famously depicted as a gigantic, three-headed dog with a serpent's tail, though some accounts describe him with fifty or a hundred heads. Cerberus is the offspring of the monsters Echidna and Typhon, and his siblings include other formidable creatures like the Lernaean Hydra and the Chimera.

Cerberus's primary role in Greek mythology is as the guardian of the gates of the Underworld, the realm of the dead ruled by Hades. His duty was to prevent the living from entering and the dead from escaping. The three heads of Cerberus are often interpreted as symbolizing the past, present, and future, as well as birth, youth, and old age, embodying the inexorable passage of time and the inevitability of death.

One of the most famous myths involving Cerberus is his capture by Heracles (Hercules) as the last of his Twelve Labors. Heracles was tasked with bringing Cerberus to the surface without using weapons. After receiving permission from Hades, Heracles overpowered Cerberus with his extraordinary strength, bringing him to King Eurystheus, and then safely returned him to the Underworld.

Cerberus's image as a fierce and formidable guardian has made him a symbol of the insurmountable boundary between the living and the dead. In ancient Greek art, he is often depicted at the side of Hades and Persephone, emphasizing his role as an integral part of the Underworld's landscape. The figure of Cerberus resonates beyond ancient myth, symbolizing the concept of a threshold guardian, a protector of a specific realm's boundaries, and the fearsome obstacles one must overcome to achieve profound transformation or transition.

Minotaur

The Minotaur is a legendary creature in Greek mythology, one of the most famous and intriguing monsters of ancient Greek lore. He is depicted as having the body of a man and the head of a bull. The Minotaur's story is tied to the island of Crete and the labyrinth that confined him.

The Minotaur was born to Pasiphaë, the wife of King Minos of Crete, and a magnificent bull. This unnatural birth was a punishment from Poseidon, whom Minos had angered by refusing to sacrifice the bull. The Minotaur, named Asterion, was a ferocious creature with an insatiable appetite for human flesh. To contain this monster, King Minos commissioned Daedalus, a skilled craftsman, to construct the Labyrinth, a complex maze from which escape was nearly impossible.

The Minotaur became central to a grim ritual involving Athens, which had been defeated by Crete. As tribute, Athens was forced to send seven young men and seven young women to Crete every nine years to be fed to the Minotaur. This continued until the arrival of Theseus, the Athenian prince. Theseus volunteered to be one of the tributes with the intent of killing the Minotaur. With the help of Ariadne, King Minos's daughter who fell in love with him, Theseus navigated the Labyrinth. Ariadne gave him a ball of thread to help him find his way back. Theseus encountered the Minotaur in the heart of the Labyrinth and, in a fierce battle, killed the beast.

The story of the Minotaur and the Labyrinth is rich in symbolic meanings and has been interpreted in various ways, from representing the struggle between reason and animalistic nature to the idea of overcoming one's inner demons. The Minotaur's image has become emblematic of the concept of the monster within a maze, a motif that resonates in various cultural and artistic expressions, symbolizing complex psychological and societal challenges. The myth encapsulates key themes of Greek mythology, including heroism, sacrifice, and the consequences of divine retribution.

Medusa

Medusa is one of the most iconic and enduring figures in Greek mythology, known for her hair of living, venomous snakes and her gaze, which turned those who looked upon her directly into stone. She was one of the three Gorgon sisters, but unlike her immortal siblings, Stheno and Euryale, Medusa was mortal.

Medusa's origins and her transformation into a Gorgon vary across myths. In one prominent version, she was originally a beautiful maiden, serving as a priestess in the temple of Athena. She was ravished by Poseidon in Athena's temple, an act which infuriated the virgin goddess. As punishment, Athena transformed Medusa's beautiful hair into serpents and made her face so terrible to behold that the mere sight of it would turn onlookers to stone. This depiction highlights the theme of victimization and unjust punishment, a common motif in Greek mythology.

Medusa's story is most famously linked to Perseus, the demigod hero. Tasked with obtaining her head, Perseus embarked on his quest with the help of divine gifts, including Hermes's winged sandals, Hades's helm of invisibility, and a reflective shield from Athena. Using the shield to avoid Medusa's direct gaze, Perseus beheaded her while she slept. From her neck sprang the winged horse Pegasus and the giant Chrysaor, products of her union with Poseidon. Perseus used Medusa's head as a weapon on several occasions before giving it to Athena, who placed it on her shield, the Aegis.

Medusa's image has transcended its mythological origins to become a symbol with varied interpretations. She embodies the terrifying, monstrous feminine, a counter to the typical damsel in distress trope common in ancient myths. Medusa's story has also been interpreted as a commentary on female rage and power, and the complexities of victimization and retribution. Her figure remains a powerful symbol in art and culture, representing a fusion of horror, beauty, and the power of the gaze.

Chimera

The Chimera is a fearsome creature in Greek mythology, renowned for its bizarre and terrifying appearance. Described as a monstrous fire-breathing hybrid, the Chimera possessed the body and head of a lion, a goat's head protruding from its back, and a serpent or dragon for a tail. This composite nature made the Chimera a symbol of the inexplicable and the monstrous, embodying the fearsome and chaotic aspects of the natural world.

The Chimera's origins are traced to the lineage of Typhon and Echidna, two monstrous figures in Greek myth, making it a sibling to other fearsome creatures like Cerberus and the Lernaean Hydra. The Chimera's story is most famously associated with the hero Bellerophon in a tale of heroism and divine favor. Bellerophon, tasked with killing the Chimera by King Iobates of Lycia, sought the help of the gods. With the aid of Athena, he captured and tamed the winged horse Pegasus. Riding Pegasus, Bellerophon was able to attack the Chimera from a safe distance, eventually slaying the beast with his spear or, in some versions, by leading it to an inescapable trap.

The Chimera's tale with Bellerophon highlights several themes common in Greek mythology, including the triumph of heroism over seemingly insurmountable challenges, and the interplay of divine intervention and human bravery. The creature itself, being an amalgamation of different animals, symbolizes the chaos and unpredictability of the natural world, and the notion that some challenges require cleverness and innovation to overcome.

In cultural and artistic depictions, the Chimera has continued to be a potent symbol of hybridity and monstrosity. Its image has been employed in various contexts to represent the combination of multiple elements into a single fearsome entity, often serving as a metaphor for complex and multifaceted challenges or threats. The Chimera remains an enduring figure in folklore, literature, and art, capturing the human fascination with the strange, the fearsome, and the wondrous.

Hydra

The Hydra, often referred to as the Lernaean Hydra, is a formidable creature in Greek mythology, famous for its role in the Twelve Labors of Heracles. It is depicted as a monstrous serpent-like creature with multiple heads — the number varies, but it is commonly said to have nine. The most terrifying aspect of the Hydra was that if one head was cut off, two more would grow in its place, making it seem almost invincible. Additionally, one of its heads was immortal, and its breath and blood were deadly poisonous.

The Hydra resided in the swamp of Lerna in the Argolid, which was considered to be an entrance to the Underworld. According to the myth, the Hydra was raised by Hera, the wife of Zeus and Heracles's divine adversary, to specifically challenge and defeat Heracles. The creature was a child of Typhon and Echidna, two of the most fearsome monsters in Greek mythology, which included other notable offspring like Cerberus and the Chimera.

Heracles's battle with the Hydra was his second labor. He journeyed to Lerna with his nephew and charioteer, Iolaus. In the battle, Heracles discovered the regenerative ability of the Hydra's heads. With Iolaus's help, he developed a strategy: as Heracles cut off each head, Iolaus cauterized the wound with a torch, preventing the growth of new heads. Once Heracles had removed all but the immortal head, he buried it under a large rock. He then dipped his arrows in the Hydra's poisonous blood, which later played a role in many of his other adventures and ultimately led to his own death.

The Hydra, in Greek mythology, symbolizes a seemingly insurmountable challenge, one that requires not just brute strength but also ingenuity and persistence to overcome. The battle with the Hydra is one of the most celebrated of Heracles's exploits and is often depicted in ancient art. The creature has become a symbol of resilience and regeneration, and its myth illustrates the concept that some challenges can grow more complex and difficult when confronted in a straightforward manner. The Hydra remains a potent symbol in popular culture, representing a formidable and complex challenge that requires clever tactics to defeat.

Cyclops

The Cyclopes (singular: Cyclops) are a group of unique and formidable characters in Greek mythology, known for their distinct single eye in the middle of their foreheads. They are often portrayed as giant, brutish beings associated with strength and craftmanship.

There are two distinct groups of Cyclopes in Greek mythology. The first group, the elder Cyclopes, were three in number: Brontes, Steropes, and Arges. They were the sons of Uranus (Sky) and Gaia (Earth), and in some myths, they are credited with forging Zeus's thunderbolts, Poseidon's trident, and Hades's helmet of invisibility. These Cyclopes were considered skilled blacksmiths and craftsmen, symbolizing the destructive and creative forces of nature.

The second and more famous group of Cyclopes is encountered in Homer's "Odyssey." These Cyclopes were pastoral giants and did not possess the same skills or attributes as the elder Cyclopes. They lived in a distant land, presumably in Sicily, in a society where each Cyclops acted independently and without regard for law or hospitality. The most famous among them is Polyphemus, who is encountered by Odysseus on his journey home from Troy. Polyphemus is portrayed as a savage, cannibalistic giant who imprisons Odysseus and his men, intending to eat them. Odysseus manages to escape by blinding

Polyphemus, after which they manage to sneak out of the cave where they were held captive.

The Cyclopes in the "Odyssey" represent the dangers of the unknown and uncivilized parts of the world, and the story of Odysseus's encounter with Polyphemus highlights themes of intelligence over brute strength, as well as the importance of hospitality—a crucial value in ancient Greek culture. The figure of the Cyclops has transcended Greek mythology, becoming a symbol of primitive strength and raw power, often depicted in various forms of art and literature, illustrating the timeless appeal of these mythological giants.

Sirens

The Sirens in Greek mythology are enchanting and dangerous creatures, renowned for their mesmerizing music and singing. According to myth, they were capable of luring sailors to their deaths with their irresistible songs. The Sirens are often depicted as having the body of a bird and the head of a woman, though in some later artistic representations, they appear as fully human, or as mermaid-like figures with the body of a woman and the tail of a fish.

The origin of the Sirens is somewhat varied in Greek mythology. One common version describes them as the daughters of the river god Achelous and a Muse (either Melpomene, the muse of tragedy, or Terpsichore, the muse of dance). Another account states they were handmaidens of Persephone, the daughter of Demeter, who were transformed by Demeter or Hera as a punishment for failing to prevent Persephone's abduction by Hades.

The most famous myth involving the Sirens occurs in Homer's "Odyssey," during Odysseus's long journey home from the Trojan War. Forewarned by the sorceress Circe about the Sirens' lethal allure, Odysseus orders his men to plug their ears with beeswax. Curious to hear the Sirens' song, Odysseus has himself tied to the mast of his ship, instructing his men not to release him no matter how much he begs. As they sail past the Sirens, Odysseus is captivated by their song, which promises to reveal all knowledge and secrets of the world. He pleads to be untied, but his loyal crew bind him tighter until they have passed out of earshot.

The Sirens in Greek mythology symbolize the perilous temptations and distractions that one might encounter on life's journey, particularly the kind that could lead one away from their intended path or duty. Their story reflects the theme of resisting temptation and the importance of knowledge and foresight in overcoming challenges. Over time, the image of the Sirens has evolved, but their association with seductive allure and the danger of the unknown remains a potent symbol in various cultural and artistic contexts.

Scylla and Charybdis

Scylla and Charybdis are two of the most infamous monsters in Greek mythology, known for their roles in Homer's "Odyssey" as formidable obstacles encountered by Odysseus on his voyage home. They are often cited together, embodying the proverbial phrase "between Scylla and Charybdis," used to describe a situation where one is faced with two opposite but equally perilous choices.

Scylla was originally a beautiful nymph who was transformed into a monstrous creature due to a jealous curse. She is depicted as having six long necks, each topped with a grisly head that contained three rows of sharp teeth. Her body consisted of twelve canine legs and a cat's tail, while six dog heads ringed her waist. She dwelled on one side of a narrow strait of water, hidden in a cave, from where she would leap out to snatch and devour sailors from passing ships.

Opposite Scylla, on the other side of the strait, resided Charybdis, another fearsome monster. Charybdis was said to be a massive whirlpool or a creature that created a whirlpool. Three times a day,

Charybdis would swallow a huge amount of water and then belch it out again, creating a whirlpool capable of dragging an entire ship underwater. According to some accounts, Charybdis was also once a beautiful nymph and was transformed into the whirlpool as a punishment by Zeus for her voracious appetite.

In the "Odyssey," Odysseus is warned by Circe about the dangers of Scylla and Charybdis. Advised that passing Scylla would be the lesser of two evils, Odysseus chooses to sail closer to her, losing a few of his men, rather than risk the loss of his entire ship to Charybdis. This episode is emblematic of the tough choices faced by Odysseus throughout his journey.

Scylla and Charybdis symbolize the inescapable dangers of the sea and the inevitability of difficult choices. Their story reflects the theme of navigating through treacherous situations, where avoiding one danger often means confronting another, just as perilous. Over time, their myth has transcended its Greek origins, becoming a metaphor for dilemmas where all options are undesirable, capturing the essence of the human condition in facing challenging decisions.

Sphinx

The Sphinx is a mythical creature in Greek mythology, known for her role in the legend of Oedipus. She is depicted as a monster with the body of a lion, the wings of a great bird, and the face of a woman. The Sphinx is most famous for her enigmatic riddle, posed to travelers who sought to enter the city of Thebes.

According to the myth, the Sphinx was sent by the gods, either as a punishment for a crime committed by the people of Thebes or as a trial. She positioned herself on the road to Thebes and posed a riddle to all who passed, devouring those who could not answer correctly. The riddle of the Sphinx was: "What is the creature that walks on four legs in the morning, two legs at noon, and three in the evening?" This riddle baffled many, leading to the demise of numerous travelers who attempted to enter the city.

The resolution of the Sphinx's riddle comes with the arrival of Oedipus, a prince of Corinth. Oedipus correctly answers that the creature is a human, who crawls on all fours as an infant, walks on two feet as an adult, and uses a walking stick in old age. Unable to bear the defeat, the Sphinx destroys herself, either by throwing herself off a rock or devouring herself, thus liberating Thebes from her reign of terror.

The Sphinx in Greek mythology symbolizes mystery, knowledge, and the power of insight. Her riddle is not just a test of cleverness, but a profound reflection on the human condition and the stages of human life. The story of the Sphinx and Oedipus is a classic example of Greek tragic literature, exploring themes of fate, destiny, and the limits of human understanding. The figure of the Sphinx has become a symbol of enigma and wisdom, her legacy enduring in various cultural and artistic representations as an emblem of the mysterious and the unknown.

Centaur

Centaurs are fascinating and distinctive creatures in Greek mythology, depicted as having the upper body of a human and the lower body and legs of a horse. These hybrid beings symbolize the dual nature of humanity, combining the civilizing aspect of humans with the untamed, instinctual nature of animals.

Centaurs were said to inhabit the mountainous regions of Thessaly and Arcadia. They were generally considered to be the offspring of Ixion, a king of the Lapiths, and Nephele, a cloud nymph created in the image of Hera. However, there are various accounts of their origins. Centaurs were often portrayed as wild and unruly, given to savage behavior and excessive indulgence in wine and revelry, though there are notable exceptions.

The most famous myth involving the centaurs is their battle with the Lapiths, which erupted during the wedding of Pirithous, king of the Lapiths, and Hippodamia. The centaurs, guests at the wedding, became drunk and tried to abduct the bride and other female guests, leading to a violent conflict known as the Centauromachy. This battle, often depicted in Greek art, symbolized the struggle between civilization and barbarism.

Among the centaurs, there were some who stood apart for their wisdom and good character. The most notable of these was Chiron, who was known for his kindness, intelligence, and skill in medicine. Chiron was a teacher and mentor to many Greek heroes, including Achilles, Asclepius, and Heracles, and was immortalized in the constellation Centaurus.

In Greek mythology, centaurs represent the inherent contradictions within human nature — the blend of civilized intellect and animalistic instinct. Their stories explore themes of coexistence and conflict between the wild and the cultured aspects of existence. The centaurs, with their dual nature, remain enduring figures in mythology, symbolizing the complex and multifaceted nature of the human condition.

Paris

Paris, also known as Alexander, is a significant figure in Greek mythology, particularly known for his role in triggering the Trojan War. He was a prince of Troy, the son of King Priam and Queen Hecuba. Before his birth, Hecuba dreamed that she gave birth to a flaming torch that consumed Troy, a prophecy interpreted as a sign that Paris would be the cause of the city's destruction.

As a result, Paris was abandoned on Mount Ida as an infant but was taken in and raised by shepherds. Unaware of his true heritage, he lived a pastoral life until his identity was revealed. Paris's most famous mythological story is his involvement in the Judgment of Paris.

Entrusted by Zeus to settle a dispute among the goddesses Hera, Athena, and Aphrodite over who was the fairest, each goddess offered him a bribe. Paris ultimately awarded the golden apple, symbolizing beauty, to Aphrodite, who promised him the most beautiful woman in the world, Helen of Sparta. This decision offended Hera and Athena and set the stage for the Trojan War.

Paris's abduction (or elopement, as some versions suggest) of Helen, who was married to King Menelaus of Sparta, led to the Greek expedition against Troy, initiating the decade-long Trojan War. In the war, Paris was not portrayed as a particularly brave or skilled warrior, in contrast to other Trojan heroes like Hector, his brother. He is often depicted as more interested in love and beauty than in fighting.

The most notable episode of Paris in the Trojan War is his killing of Achilles. Guided by Apollo, Paris shot an arrow that struck Achilles' only vulnerable spot, his heel, leading to the death of the greatest Greek warrior. Paris himself was eventually killed during the war, fulfilling the prophecy of Troy's downfall being linked to him.

Paris's character in Greek mythology is complex, often seen as a symbol of the consequences of poor judgment and the devastating effects of personal desires over communal well-being. His story, particularly the Judgment of Paris and the abduction of Helen, highlights themes of choice, beauty, and the catastrophic ripple effects of individual actions in the realm of human destiny.

Agamemnon

Agamemnon is a pivotal figure in Greek mythology, most famous for his role as the king of Mycenae and the commander-in-chief of the Greek forces in the Trojan War. He is a central character in several ancient Greek tragedies and epics, notably in Homer's "Iliad" and in plays by Aeschylus and Euripides. Agamemnon was the son of King Atreus of Mycenae and Queen Aerope, and the brother of Menelaus, the king of Sparta.

Agamemnon's involvement in the Trojan War began with the abduction (or elopement) of Helen, the wife of his brother Menelaus, by Paris of Troy. Agamemnon led the Greek coalition in the ensuing war, which lasted ten years. His leadership was marked by both brilliance and controversy. He was a powerful warrior and strategist, but his tenure as commander was fraught with discord, particularly his conflict with Achilles over the captive woman Briseis, which is a central plot in the "Iliad." This quarrel led to Achilles' withdrawal from battle, significantly impacting the course of the war.

One of the most infamous episodes involving Agamemnon occurred at the outset of the Trojan War. To appease the goddess Artemis, who had stilled the winds to prevent the Greek fleet from sailing to Troy, Agamemnon sacrificed his daughter Iphigenia. This act set off a chain of tragic events that would culminate in his own death.

After the fall of Troy, Agamemnon returned home to Mycenae, where he was murdered by his wife, Clytemnestra, and her lover, Aegisthus. Clytemnestra's act was partly in revenge for the sacrifice of Iphigenia and partly due to her relationship with Aegisthus. Agamemnon's death and the subsequent revenge by his son, Orestes, form the basis of the Oresteia, a trilogy of plays by Aeschylus.

Agamemnon's story is one of power, pride, and tragic downfall, encapsulating the themes of hubris, the costs of ambition, and the complex interplay of personal and familial loyalties. His character is a study in the strengths and weaknesses of leadership, the moral ambiguities of war, and the inexorable nature of fate and retributive justice in Greek mythology.

Menelaus

Menelaus is a notable figure in Greek mythology, primarily recognized as the king of Sparta and a central character in the story of the Trojan War. He is the son of Atreus, the king of Mycenae, and Aerope, and the younger brother of Agamemnon, who led the Greek forces against Troy. Menelaus's role in Greek myth is deeply intertwined with the events leading up to and during the Trojan War.

Menelaus became king of Sparta through his marriage to Helen, considered the most beautiful woman in the world. Their marriage was a significant event, attended by many notable figures, including Odysseus. To secure Helen's hand, Menelaus had to agree to support her previous suitor, should she ever need protection. This agreement played a crucial role in the events that followed.

The pivotal moment in Menelaus's life and in Greek mythology was the abduction (or elopement) of Helen by Paris, a prince of Troy. This act was considered a grave insult and betrayal, prompting Menelaus to call upon the other Greek kings and princes, who had sworn the oath, to help him retrieve Helen. This led to the assembly of a massive Greek expedition and the onset of the Trojan War, a ten-year siege of the city of Troy.

During the Trojan War, as depicted in Homer's "Iliad," Menelaus is portrayed as a brave and competent warrior, though not as prominent as heroes like Achilles or Hector. His duel with Paris is one of the memorable episodes in the war, highlighting his desire for revenge and justice. After the fall of Troy, Menelaus reclaimed Helen and returned to Sparta, where they lived together again.

Menelaus's character in mythology explores themes of honor, revenge, and the complexities of marital and political alliances. His pursuit of Helen and involvement in the Trojan War exemplify the interplay of personal motives and broader political and military actions in ancient Greek lore. Menelaus, while overshadowed by more prominent heroes of the Trojan War, remains an essential figure in the saga, representing the human costs of pride, betrayal, and the pursuit of restitution.

Priam

Priam, in Greek mythology, is a pivotal figure best known as the venerable king of Troy during the Trojan War. He is a central character in many stories and plays, most notably in Homer's "Iliad." Priam was the son of Laomedon, the previous king of Troy, and was originally named Podarces. He assumed the name Priam, which means "redeemed," after being spared by Heracles during the sack of Troy and ransoming his own life with a golden veil.

Priam's reign as king of Troy was marked by prosperity and wealth, but it is most remembered for the Greek siege of the city that lasted a decade. The war began following the abduction of Helen by Paris, Priam's son, an act that sparked the conflict between Troy and the coalition of Greek forces led by King Agamemnon. Despite his old age, Priam played a significant role in the war, primarily as a wise and compassionate ruler, deeply affected by the suffering the war brought to his family and his people.

One of the most poignant moments in the "Iliad" involves Priam's visit to Achilles' tent to beg for the return of the body of his son Hector, who was slain by Achilles in revenge for the death of Achilles' close friend Patroclus. The encounter between the aged king and the formidable warrior is a powerful scene that highlights themes of shared humanity, grief, and respect for the dead, transcending the enmity and rage of war.

Priam's tragic end comes with the fall of Troy, where he is killed by Neoptolemus, the son of Achilles. His death signifies not only the personal tragedy of a father who lost many of his sons in the war but also the broader downfall of a once-great city and culture. Priam's character in Greek mythology embodies the dignity, sorrows, and vulnerabilities of a ruler facing the ultimate destruction of his city and family. His portrayal in the "Iliad" and other works offers deep insights into the themes of leadership, the ravages of war, and the profound impacts of personal and political decisions.

Andromache

Andromache is a poignant and respected figure in Greek mythology, known primarily for her role in Homer's "Iliad" as the loyal and sorrowful wife of Hector, the prince of Troy and the city's greatest warrior during the Trojan War. She is presented as an epitome of spousal devotion and maternal anguish, her character embodying the tragic impact of war on women and families.

Andromache was the daughter of Eetion, the king of Cilician Thebe, and thus of noble lineage. She married Hector, and together they had a son, Astyanax. Her life in Troy was marked by the shadow of the impending Greek siege, and her portrayal in the "Iliad" is most memorable for the tender and tragic scenes with Hector, particularly their final parting. In these moments, Andromache expresses profound grief and premonitions about the grim fate awaiting Troy and her family, fearing the loss of her husband and the future enslavement and suffering of herself and her son.

Her fears tragically come true with Hector's death at the hands of Achilles. Following the fall of Troy, Andromache's son Astyanax is brutally killed, and she becomes a war prize of Neoptolemus, Achilles' son. The later myths and plays describe her life in captivity, her marriage to Neoptolemus, and eventually, her marriage to Helenus, Hector's brother, after Neoptolemus's death.

Andromache's character in Greek mythology and literature is a profound portrayal of the suffering of those left behind in war — the wives, mothers, and children.

Penelope

Penelope is a central figure in Greek mythology, renowned for her loyalty, patience, and ingenuity. She is best known from Homer's "Odyssey," where she is depicted as the faithful wife of the hero Odysseus, awaiting his return from the Trojan War. Penelope was the daughter of Icarius of Sparta and the cousin of Helen of Troy. She married Odysseus, the king of Ithaca, and together they had a son, Telemachus.

During the ten-year-long Trojan War and Odysseus's subsequent ten-year-long journey home, Penelope remained in Ithaca, where she faced the constant pressure of suitors. These suitors, believing Odysseus to be dead, sought her hand in marriage, each hoping to claim the throne of Ithaca. Penelope, however, remained steadfast in her belief that Odysseus was still alive and would return.

Penelope is most famous for her ruse of weaving a shroud during the day and unraveling it at night, thereby delaying her decision to remarry. She promised the suitors that she would choose a new husband once she finished weaving the shroud for her father-in-law, Laertes. This trick bought Odysseus enough time to return home after his long odyssey.

Penelope's reunion with Odysseus is a climax of the "Odyssey." She initially does not recognize him, as he is disguised as a beggar. It is only after he passes a test she devises — to string Odysseus's great bow and shoot an arrow through twelve axe heads — that she believes his identity. Even then, she tests him further to ensure he truly is her long-lost husband.

Penelope's character in the "Odyssey" is complex and multifaceted. She embodies the ideals of marital fidelity, patience in adversity, and cunning intelligence. Her steadfastness and cleverness make her an integral counterpart to Odysseus, paralleling his own journey with her struggles at home. Penelope's story has been interpreted in various ways, from a testament to the strength and agency of a loyal wife to a commentary on the hardships faced by those left behind during war. Her legacy in literature and art has made her an enduring symbol of devotion and resilience.

Hector

Hector is one of the most noble and revered characters in Greek mythology, particularly renowned for his role in Homer's epic, the "Iliad." He was a prince of Troy and the greatest warrior for the Trojans during the Trojan War, often portrayed as the embodiment of the ideal warrior and a symbol of devotion to family and country.

As the eldest son of King Priam and Queen Hecuba of Troy, Hector was not only a prince but also the city's main defender. His wife was Andromache, with whom he had a son, Astyanax. Hector's character is marked by his sense of duty, honor, and his deep commitment to the welfare of his city and his family. Unlike many of his fellow Trojans, Hector was known for his level-headedness and sense of responsibility.

In the "Iliad," Hector is a central figure, leading the defense of Troy against the Greek invaders. His most notable battles include conflicts with Ajax and Patroclus (Achilles's close friend and companion), the latter of whom he kills in battle, unaware that Patroclus is wearing Achilles's armor. Hector's slaying of Patroclus ultimately leads to his own death at the hands of Achilles, who seeks revenge. The scenes of Hector's farewell to his wife and son, and his death, are among the most poignant in the "Iliad," highlighting the tragic human cost of the war.

Hector's death marks a turning point in the Trojan War. His body is initially dishonored by Achilles, who drags it behind his chariot, but eventually, King Priam begs Achilles for Hector's body so he can be given a proper funeral. Moved by Priam's plea, Achilles agrees, and Hector is mourned by both Trojans and Greeks.

Hector stands out in Greek mythology as a figure of integrity and valor, often contrasted with Achilles as a foil: Hector the dutiful defender of his city and family, and Achilles the unrivaled warrior driven by personal glory and revenge. Hector's legacy is that of the tragic hero, embodying the virtues of honor, loyalty, and the protective spirit of a warrior who fights not for personal glory, but for the people he loves and the city he is bound to defend.

Patroclus

Patroclus is a significant figure in Greek mythology, known for his close companionship with Achilles, the greatest warrior in Homer's "Iliad." His story is central to the narrative of the Trojan War and plays a crucial role in the unfolding of events leading to the fall of Troy.

Patroclus was the son of Menoetius, a friend of King Peleus and the sea nymph Thetis, Achilles' parents. His upbringing was intertwined with that of Achilles, and they grew up together, forming a deep bond of friendship. In some versions of the myth, Patroclus was exiled from his home for accidentally killing a boy during a game, after which he was taken in by Peleus and raised alongside Achilles.

In the "Iliad," Patroclus is portrayed as a brave and capable warrior, although he is overshadowed by Achilles's prowess. During the Trojan War, when Achilles withdrew from battle due to his quarrel with Agamemnon over the maiden Briseis, it was Patroclus who, seeing the Greeks losing ground, donned Achilles's armor and led the Myrmidons into combat. His actions temporarily turned the tide against the Trojans.

Patroclus's most significant and tragic role in the myth is his death at the hands of Hector, the Trojan prince and hero. Believing Patroclus to be Achilles because of the armor he wore, Hector killed him in battle. Patroclus's death had profound implications: it spurred Achilles to return to the fight, seeking vengeance against Hector, which ultimately led to Hector's death and the turning point in the Trojan War.

The relationship between Achilles and Patroclus has been a subject of great interest and varying interpretations throughout history. In ancient times, they were often seen as exemplars of deep and loyal friendship. Later interpretations, including those in modern literature and scholarship, have explored the possibility of a romantic relationship between the two.

Patroclus's character and his relationship with Achilles highlight themes of loyalty, the consequences of pride, and the personal cost of war. His death is one of the most poignant moments in the "Iliad," underscoring the human tragedy and complexity at the heart of the epic. Patroclus remains a symbol of the deep bonds that can form between comrades-in-arms and the profound impact such relationships can have on historical events.

Ajax

Ajax, also known as Ajax the Great, is a prominent figure in Greek mythology, celebrated for his stature as a mighty warrior in the Trojan War. He is a key character in Homer's "Iliad" and features in various other mythological narratives and tragedies. There were actually two Greek heroes named Ajax who fought in the Trojan War; the more famous one, Ajax the Great, was the son of Telamon, king of Salamis, making him a prince. The other, Ajax the Lesser, was the son of Oileus, king of Locris.

Ajax the Great was known for his enormous size and strength, second only to Achilles in prowess among the Greek warriors at Troy. He was described as a towering and formidable figure, wielding a huge shield made of seven cowhides with a layer of bronze. Ajax played a crucial role in the Trojan War, participating in numerous battles and duels, including a famous combat with Hector, prince of Troy. Although the duel ended in a stalemate, Ajax earned respect from both the Greek and Trojan sides for his valor.

One of the most significant moments in Ajax's story is in the aftermath of Achilles' death. Ajax and Odysseus both competed for the armor of Achilles, which was to be awarded to the bravest Greek warrior. When the armor was awarded to Odysseus, Ajax was driven into a furious rage. According to some versions of the myth, this rage led to his death – not at the hands of the Trojans, but through his own actions. In a fit of madness, induced by Athena, Ajax slaughtered a flock of sheep, believing them to be his enemies. Upon regaining his senses and realizing what he had done, he was consumed with shame and fell on his own sword, choosing death over living with the disgrace.

Ajax the Great's character embodies the classical Greek heroic ideals of strength and bravery, but his story also serves as a cautionary tale about pride, honor, and the psychological burdens of warfare. His tragic end highlights the often-overlooked human aspect of the legendary heroes of Greek mythology, revealing vulnerabilities and inner conflicts amidst their celebrated feats. Ajax's legacy in mythology and literature underscores the complexity of heroism and the profound personal costs of war.

The Muses

The Muses are iconic figures in Greek mythology, revered as the goddesses of the arts, literature, and sciences. They are traditionally nine in number, each representing a different realm of creativity and intellectual endeavor. The Muses are considered the sources of knowledge and inspiration for poets, musicians, and artists. They were believed to bestow the gift of creativity and to provide the divine spark for artistic and intellectual creation.

The Muses are daughters of Zeus, the king of the gods, and Mnemosyne, the Titaness of memory. This parentage symbolizes the union of divine authority with the power of memory and the past, underpinning the importance of the Muses in the transmission of knowledge and culture. They were typically worshipped in the proximity of the sacred Mount Olympus, and they were associated with the spring of Pieria, a place that was believed to be a source of inspiration.

Each of the nine Muses presides over a different art form or scientific discipline:

Calliope: The Muse of epic poetry and eloquence. She is often depicted holding a writing tablet.

Clio: The Muse of history, depicted with a scroll or a book.

Erato: The Muse of love poetry and lyric poetry, often seen with a lyre.

Euterpe: The Muse of music, especially flute playing.

Melpomene: The Muse of tragedy, traditionally holding the tragic mask.

Polyhymnia: The Muse of sacred poetry, hymns, and eloquence; often shown in a thoughtful pose.

Terpsichore: The Muse of dance and choral song, frequently depicted with a lyre and in a dancing pose.

Thalia: The Muse of comedy and idyllic poetry, often portrayed with the comic mask.

Urania: The Muse of astronomy and astrology, usually represented with a globe.

In Greek culture, the Muses were invoked at the beginning of poems, songs, and sagas, as poets and bards sought their inspiration and blessings for their endeavors. They were not only central to the artistic and intellectual pursuits of the Greeks but also served as symbols of the pursuit of knowledge and the importance of remembering and celebrating the past. The concept of the Muses has endured throughout Western culture as a representation of artistic inspiration and creativity, influencing countless works of art, literature, and music across the ages.

The Fates

In Greek mythology, the Fates, also known as the Moirai, are a group of three deities who control the destiny of both mortals and gods. Their role is to ensure that every being follows their predestined path in life, which was believed to be woven by them at the birth of each individual. The Fates are often depicted as stern, unyielding, and impartial figures, overseeing the fundamental order of the cosmos and the inevitable cycle of birth, life, and death.

The three Fates are:

Clotho ("the spinner"): She is responsible for spinning the thread of life, essentially starting the life of every individual. She symbolizes the beginning of life and is often depicted with a spindle.

Lachesis ("the allotter"): Her role is to measure the thread of life, determining the length and thus the lifespan and destiny of the individual. Lachesis represents the unfolding of one's life path and is usually shown with a measuring rod or a scroll.

Atropos ("the unturnable" or "inevitable"): She is the one who cuts the thread of life, determining the moment of death for every being. Atropos represents the finality of death and is often depicted with a pair of scissors or a sharp blade.

In Greek mythology, the Fates are daughters of Nyx (Night) in some traditions, while in others, they are said to be offspring of Zeus and Themis or of Ananke (Necessity). Regardless of their parentage, they are portrayed as older women, and their decisions are not to be questioned or interfered with, even by the gods. The Fates play a crucial role in many Greek myths, where their decrees are often a central element of the narrative, demonstrating the limitations of even the most powerful gods and heroes in the face of destiny.

The concept of the Fates underscores the ancient Greek belief in the predetermined nature of existence and the limited scope of individual agency against the universal laws of fate and destiny. Their presence in mythology and literature highlights the inevitability of life's journey and the natural cycle of birth, life, and death. The Fates remain a potent symbol of the mysterious forces that govern the world and the human condition, embodying the idea that certain aspects of life are beyond human control.

The Nymphs

In Greek mythology, nymphs are minor female deities associated with nature, typically depicted as beautiful, young maidens inhabiting rivers, woods, trees, mountains, meadows, and seas. They are considered to be divine spirits who animate nature, often regarded as the personification of the creative and nurturing aspects of nature. Nymphs are generally benevolent, interacting with gods and humans, and are known for their playful, free-spirited nature.

Nymphs are categorized according to the specific aspect of nature they represent. Some of the main types of nymphs include:

Naiads: Freshwater nymphs dwelling in springs, rivers, brooks, and lakes. They were thought to be responsible for the nurturing of plant life and were closely associated with particular bodies of water.

Dryads and Hamadryads: Forest and tree nymphs. Dryads were connected with forests and groves, while Hamadryads were born with a certain tree and shared its fate.

Oreads: Mountain nymphs, inhabiting and personifying the features of mountains and hills.

Nereids and Oceanids: Sea nymphs, with the Nereids associated with the Mediterranean Sea and the Oceanids linked with the vast ocean. They were often depicted as companions of the sea god Poseidon.

Meliae: Nymphs associated with ash trees, often linked to the nurturing of children and the earth.

Nymphs feature in many mythological stories and are often associated with particular gods and heroes. They could be both nurturing and dangerous; for example, the Naiads could cause floods, and the Dryads could punish those who harmed their trees. Nymphs often took part in the retinue of gods, such as Artemis, the goddess of the hunt, and Dionysus, the god of wine and ecstasy.

The mythology of nymphs reflects the ancient Greeks' reverence for the natural world and their belief in the presence of divine entities within the landscape. Nymphs symbolize the life-giving and fertile aspects of nature, as well as the allure and mystery of the natural world. They have been a popular subject in art and literature, embodying the grace and beauty of nature in a humanized form.

Satyrs

Satyrs are mythical creatures in Greek mythology, known for their wild, uninhibited nature, and often associated with Dionysus, the god of wine, fertility, and ritualistic ecstasy. They are depicted as beings with human upper bodies and the lower bodies of goats, including features like pointed ears, tails, and sometimes a horse's mane and tail.

Satyrs represent the untamed, instinctual aspects of nature, embodying the primal forces of the wilderness and the earth's fertility. They are often portrayed in myths and artworks as followers of Dionysus, indulging in revelries, dancing, and playing music, especially the pan flute. Their behavior is typically characterized by lasciviousness, merriment, and a lack of concern for convention or decorum, reflecting the uninhibited characteristics associated with Dionysian rituals.

One of the most prominent satyrs in Greek mythology is Pan, the god of the wild, shepherds, and flocks, often identified as the chief of the satyrs. Another notable satyr is Silenus, a companion and tutor to Dionysus, typically depicted as an older, wiser, but still drunken figure.

In the context of Greek culture and mythology, satyrs embody the concept of man's inherent connection to nature and the animalistic side of his nature. They serve as a counterpoint to the civilized aspects of Greek society, representing a world removed from societal norms and restrictions. Their presence in mythological narratives often highlights themes of revelry, fertility, and the natural cycle of life and death, as well as the allure and danger of the wild.

Over time, the portrayal of satyrs has evolved. In classical art, they were often depicted as quite beastly and grotesque, but during the Hellenistic period, their depiction became more humanized. The satyr has remained a popular figure in art and literature, symbolizing the untamed, primal aspects of the world and the allure of a life uninhibited by societal constraints.

The Graces

The Graces, also known as the Charites in Greek mythology, are a trio of goddesses who embody grace, beauty, and charm, and are associated with the aspects of creativity, fertility, and the joy of life. They are often depicted as three beautiful, ethereal young women who are sisters, dancing together in a circle.

The Graces are generally named as:

Aglaea (Splendor): The youngest of the three, she is sometimes considered to represent the glow of good health or beauty.

Euphrosyne (Mirth): She embodies the aspects of joy, mirth, and merriment.

Thalia (Good Cheer): Not to be confused with Thalia the Muse, this Thalia represents festivity and rich banquets.

The Graces are the daughters of Zeus, the king of the gods, and Eurynome, an Oceanid, or, in some accounts, Dionysus and Aphrodite. They are often found in the retinue of other gods and goddesses, including Aphrodite, the goddess of love, and Apollo, the god of music and the arts. Their presence was believed to enhance the other gods' powers and bring a sense of harmony and joy to both divine and mortal realms.

In art and literature, the Graces are often depicted as providing their blessings to mortals and gods alike. They represent the bestowing of creativity, beauty, and charm, and are often invoked in poetry and artistic endeavors. They also symbolize the pleasant aspects of nature and life, contributing to an environment of harmony, good cheer, and amiability.

The Graces played a subtle but important role in Greek mythology and culture. They were seen as the personification of beauty and graciousness, both in nature and in human life. The reverence for the Graces reflected the Greek appreciation for the finer aspects of life, including art, beauty, and social festivities, underlining the importance of balance and joy in the human experience. Their enduring legacy can be seen in the way these concepts are still valued and pursued in various forms of art and cultural expressions today.

Chapter 4: Creation Myth

In the nascent whispers of time, before the world as we know it took shape, there existed only Chaos – a vast, yawning void. It was not merely an empty space, but a primordial state of existence, formless and infinite. From this chasm of nothingness and silence, the first entities began to emerge, not through the designs of a creator, but as if by the inevitable hand of necessity.

The earliest born from Chaos was Gaia, the Earth, a solid foundation arising from the nonentity. She was not merely the physical earth but a living, breathing deity – the mother of all life. Gaia's emergence brought definition to the world, a contrast to the unfathomable emptiness of Chaos. She was majestic and nurturing, her vastness encompassing all the potential of terrestrial existence.

Accompanying Gaia in these earliest moments were other primordial forces. There was Tartarus, the dark abyss that lay deep within the bowels of the earth, a dungeon of torment and suffering for those who would later cross the gods. From Chaos also came Eros, the embodiment of love and procreation, an essential force for the continuation of life and the inevitable intermingling of beings. Erebus, the personification of darkness, and Nyx, the night, emerged, enveloping the nascent world in their shadowy veil, creating a cycle of day and night, light and dark.

Gaia, in her solitude, yearned for a companion and thus brought forth Uranus, the sky, to cover her, creating a union between earth and heavens. Uranus became her husband, and together they began the first dynasty of the world. From their union came the Titans, a race of powerful and gigantic beings. Among these were Oceanus, who encircled the world, and his sister Tethys; Hyperion and Theia, whose children would be the sun and the moon; as well as Rhea, Themis, Mnemosyne, and Cronus, the youngest and most ambitious of the Titans.

But not all that Gaia and Uranus created was harmonious and fair. Uranus, fearing the power of his children, imprisoned Gaia's other offspring: the Cyclopes – one-eyed giants skilled in craftsmanship – and the Hecatoncheires, hundred-handed giants of incredible strength and ferocity. Gaia mourned the loss of her children and raged against Uranus for his cruelty.

The world, initially born from serenity and union, now echoed with the seeds of conflict and strife. It was within this tumultuous landscape that the narrative of the gods, of heroes and monsters, of triumphs and tragedies, began to unfold. The stage was set for a saga that would shape the very fabric of existence, a story of power, betrayal, love, and retribution.

Thus, from the void of Chaos, the world and its ancient inhabitants came into being, a testament to the complexity and depth of Greek mythology.

Chapter 5: The Titanomachy

In the annals of ancient Greek mythos, few tales rivaled the grandeur and significance of the Titanomachy, the great war between the Titans, the old gods, and the Olympians, the new deities who sought to overthrow the ancient order. This cataclysmic conflict, steeped in power struggles and divine drama, marked the end of one era and the dawn of another.

The seeds of this celestial war were sown by the Titan Cronus, who had usurped his father Uranus, the Sky, to become the ruler of the cosmos. Fearing a prophecy that he would be overthrown by his own offspring, Cronus swallowed his children as they were born. This dark act of desperation haunted his reign, casting a shadow over his dominion.

Rhea, Cronus's wife and sister, anguished by the loss of her children, conceived a plan to save her youngest, Zeus. She hid Zeus away in a cave on the island of Crete, entrusting his upbringing to the nymphs and the spirits of the mountain. In the shelter of this hidden sanctuary, Zeus grew in power and strength, nurtured by the milk of the goat Amalthea and the protective songs of the warriors of the Curetes.

Upon reaching maturity, Zeus, guided by Gaia, sought to challenge the tyranny of Cronus. The young god secured the aid of Metis, a daughter of Oceanus, who provided him with an emetic potion. Disguised as a cupbearer, Zeus served Cronus this potion, causing the Titan to vomit forth the swallowed siblings of Zeus – Hestia, Demeter, Hera, Hades, and Poseidon – who were still alive, undigested, and eager for retribution.

The stage was set for a cosmic upheaval. Zeus, leading his liberated siblings and allies, declared war against Cronus and the ruling Titans. The Olympians, representing a new order, stood for change and evolution, while the Titans, under Cronus, clung to the old ways, the ancient regime. The two sides amassed their forces, with the Titans fortifying themselves on Mount Othrys, and the Olympians rallying on Mount Olympus.

The war that ensued was monumental and earth-shattering, lasting a decade, with neither side gaining a clear advantage. The Olympians, though younger and more vigorous, were initially inexperienced in combat. The Titans, older and more seasoned, were formidable in their might. The battles were ferocious, with the skies thundering and the earth quaking as these powerful beings clashed.

It was Prometheus, a Titan known for his foresight, who first defected to the Olympian cause, foreseeing their eventual victory. Zeus also freed the Cyclopes and the Hecatoncheires, the hundred-handed giants, from their imprisonment in Tartarus. In gratitude, the Cyclopes bestowed upon Zeus his signature weapon, the thunderbolt, and gave other powerful gifts to his siblings.

The tide of war turned when the Hecatoncheires joined the fray, hurling massive rocks with their hundred hands and overwhelming the Titans with their brute force. Zeus, in his divine fury, hurled thunderbolts with unerring precision, wreaking havoc upon the Titan ranks.

In the final, decisive moments of the war, Zeus unleashed his full might, assisted by his siblings and allies. The heavens roared and the earth burned as the Olympians displayed their raw power. Cronus and his Titan allies, unable to withstand this onslaught, were eventually subdued.

The aftermath of the Titanomachy saw the vanquished Titans banished to the depths of Tartarus, a dark, dismal pit in the furthest reaches of the earth, where they would be imprisoned forever, far from the light of the world. The Hecatoncheires were appointed their guards, ensuring their eternal confinement.

With the fall of the Titans, Zeus and his siblings established a new order, with Zeus becoming the supreme ruler of the cosmos. The Olympian deities, each embodying different aspects of the world and human experience, took their place in the newly formed pantheon, overseeing the realms of the heavens, the earth, and the sea.

Thus concluded the Titanomachy, a foundational myth representing the struggle between the old order and the new, a theme resonant in the human experience. It was a tale of ambition, power, betrayal, and the inexorable march of time and change – themes that would echo through the ages in the rich tapestry of Greek mythology.

Chapter 6: The 12 Labors of Heracles

Heracles, born to the mortal woman Alcmene and the king of gods, Zeus, was a figure marked by divine favor and mortal enmity from his very inception. His mere existence was a result of Zeus's infidelity, a recurring theme in the god's numerous liaisons. Hera, the queen of the gods and Zeus's wife, upon learning of this betrayal, was consumed with jealousy and hatred towards the illegitimate offspring of her unfaithful husband.

Heracles, whose name means "Glory of Hera," was to bear the brunt of the goddess's wrath throughout his life. As an infant, he demonstrated his extraordinary strength by strangling two serpents sent by Hera to kill him in his cradle. Yet, his physical prowess was no shield against the psychological torments he would later endure.

The pivotal moment that led to the Twelve Labors occurred when Hera, exploiting her divine powers, struck Heracles with a temporary madness. In a tragic twist of fate, this bout of insanity led Heracles to commit the most grievous of acts: the slaying of his own wife, Megara, and their children. Upon recovering his senses and realizing the atrocity he had committed, Heracles was engulfed in a maelstrom of guilt and despair. His actions, although unintended, necessitated atonement of the highest order.

Seeking purification and redemption, Heracles consulted the Oracle of Delphi, the most revered source of divine wisdom. The Oracle, guided by the machinations of Hera, commanded him to serve King Eurystheus of Tiryns – a man known for neither his bravery nor his virtue, but one whom Hera favored. It was Eurystheus who imposed the Twelve Labors upon Heracles, each task an endeavor of increasing difficulty and peril, designed to test the limits of his strength, courage, and cunning.

The story of Heracles and his Twelve Labors is more than a tale of adventures and mythical beasts; it is a narrative of resilience in the face of adversity, the quest for redemption, and the struggle to redefine one's legacy. As we embark on this journey alongside Heracles, we delve into a saga that has captivated the human imagination for millennia, reminding us that even in our darkest hour, the potential for redemption and greatness lies within.

Labor 1 – The Nemean Lion

Heracles' first Labor set forth by King Eurystheus was to confront and vanquish the Nemean Lion, a creature of such formidable might and fearsome reputation that its very name stirred whispers of dread. Nestled in the shadowy hills of Nemea, the lion roamed, its hide impervious to the weapons of man, a living embodiment of nature's untamed and brutal force.

As Heracles ventured into the rugged landscape of Nemea, the air was heavy with anticipation, the sun casting long shadows over the land that had become the lion's hunting ground. The tales of the lion's invincibility had reached far and wide, yet Heracles, undeterred, pushed forward, driven by a resolve that was as much a part of him as his legendary strength.

Upon reaching the lion's den, a cavernous maw in the side of a hill, Heracles found himself enveloped in an almost palpable silence, broken only by the distant sound of the wind weaving through the olive groves. He entered the lair, his eyes adjusting to the pressing darkness, every sense heightened.

The encounter with the Nemean Lion was a clash of titanic forces. Heracles quickly discovered that his weapons were useless against the beast's enchanted hide. It became a battle of raw strength and primal instinct. They grappled ferociously, Heracles matching the lion's savage blows with his own brute force. In the end, it was with his bare hands that Heracles overcame the beast, choking the lion to death.

He skinned the lion using its own claws and donned its hide, a symbol of his victory and a testament to the indomitable spirit that would guide him through the subsequent labors. Heracles then returned to the king, but the sight of Heracles wearing the lion's hide, its head still attached as a fearsome helmet, was too daunting a spectacle for Eurystheus. The king, who had expected the Nemean Lion to be an insurmountable challenge for Heracles, was both astonished and terrified by the hero's success. In some versions of the myth, Eurystheus was so intimidated by Heracles' fearsome appearance clad in the lion's skin that he hid in a specially constructed bronze jar, refusing to come out to meet Heracles directly.

Labor 2 – The Lernaean Hydra

The second Labor of Heracles, as decreed by King Eurystheus, took him to the swamps near the ancient city of Lerna. His mission: to vanquish the Lernaean Hydra, a lethal, many-headed serpent whose mere breath could be deadly. This creature, born from Typhon and Echidna, posed a unique challenge, for it was said that if one of its heads were severed, two more would sprout in its place.

The Hydra resided in the depths of a murky, fetid swamp, shrouded in mists that twisted like wraiths in the dim light. As Heracles approached, he could feel the malice in the air, a palpable presence that weighed heavily upon his shoulders. With him was his loyal nephew, Iolaus, who would prove to be indispensable in the ordeal that lay ahead.

Heracles, undaunted by the task, waded into the swamp, his presence disturbing the eerie stillness. The Hydra, sensing an intruder, emerged from the fetid waters with a fearsome hiss, its many heads weaving menacingly. The battle that ensued was one of both strength and strategy. Heracles soon realized that merely cutting off the heads of the Hydra was futile; as each head fell, two more took its place, the creature becoming even more formidable.

In the heat of battle, it was Iolaus who provided the crucial insight. He suggested using fire to cauterize the stumps after each decapitation, thus preventing the regeneration of the heads. Working in tandem, Heracles sliced off each head, while Iolaus, wielding a torch, seared the wounds closed. Together, they systematically reduced the number of snarling heads, Heracles' sword flashing and Iolaus' torch blazing.

The Hydra had one immortal head that was impervious to Heracles' attacks. With a mighty effort, Heracles severed this final head and, following the guidance of Athena, buried it under a massive rock, ensuring it would never trouble the world again. As a final act of cunning, Heracles dipped his arrows in the Hydra's venomous blood, imbuing them with lethal power for future endeavors.

Labor 3 – The Ceryneian Hind

The third Labor set before Heracles by King Eurystheus was a task of stealth and speed, markedly different from the brute force required in his previous challenges. He was commanded to capture the Ceryneian Hind, a creature as elusive as it was magnificent. This was no ordinary animal; it was a radiant hind, sacred to Artemis, the goddess of the hunt, famed for its golden antlers and hooves of bronze. Moreover, it was not just swift but supernaturally fleet-footed, capable of outrunning an arrow in flight.

The Ceryneian Hind roamed the woods of Ceryneia, and capturing such a creature was a task that seemed to border on the impossible. Heracles, aware of the hind's divine significance, knew that he must undertake this labor with care to avoid the wrath of

Artemis. He set out on a year-long pursuit, a relentless chase that tested the limits of his endurance and persistence.

The chase led Heracles through dense forests, across rugged mountains, and along the banks of rushing rivers. He pushed forward, his determination unwavering, despite the elusiveness of his quarry. The hind, with its supernatural speed, was always just beyond reach, its golden antlers glinting in the sunlight as it bounded effortlessly through the wilderness.

After a year of pursuit, Heracles finally resorted to a direct approach. He waited until the hind was resting and managed to catch it off guard, ensnaring it with a skillfully thrown net, or, in some versions of the myth, wounding it gently with an arrow. The capture, however, did not go unnoticed by Artemis, who, along with her brother Apollo, confronted Heracles.

In a tense exchange, Heracles pleaded his case, explaining the compulsion of the labors imposed upon him and his intent to return the hind unharmed. His respect and eloquence swayed the goddess, who, recognizing the will of fate and Heracles' devotion to his task, allowed him to take the hind to Eurystheus, with the understanding that it would be returned to her care.

Labor 4 – The Erymanthian Boar

The fourth Labor of Heracles, as decreed by King Eurystheus, tasked the hero with a challenge of a different nature, one that tested not only his strength but his cunning and resilience against nature's formidable forces. His mission was to capture the Erymanthian Boar, a monstrous creature known for its immense size, ferocious temperament, and the havoc it wreaked upon the region of Erymanthia.

Unlike his previous endeavors, this task required a blend of strategic hunting skills and raw power. The Erymanthian Boar was no ordinary animal; it was a beast of mythical proportions, rampaging through the forests and mountains, uprooting trees and terrifying the inhabitants of the region. Its tusks were like scythes, and its breath was as hot and fierce as the winds of a storm.

Heracles set out for Mount Erymanthus, armed with his bow, club, and indomitable spirit. The journey itself was treacherous, taking him through dense, thorny underbrush and steep, craggy paths. As he ventured deeper into the wilderness, the signs of the boar's presence grew more evident – trees uprooted, the earth torn asunder, the air filled with an ominous sense of dread.

Upon locating the boar, Heracles engaged in a deadly game of pursuit. Heracles, relying on his agility and tactical acumen, evaded the creature's deadly assaults, wearing it down through a relentless chase. The climax of this labor occurred in a deep, snow-laden valley. Heracles cleverly drove the exhausted beast into the thick snow, which hindered its movements and sapped its strength. Seizing the opportunity, Heracles ensnared the boar in a net, showcasing not only his physical prowess but also his ability to adapt and outthink his opponent.

With the Erymanthian Boar finally in his grasp, Heracles embarked on the arduous journey back to Mycenae. The sight of the weary but triumphant hero, dragging the immense boar behind him, was one that captured the imagination of all who witnessed it. To Eurystheus, the presentation of the live boar was a source of both awe and fear – another undeniable testament to Heracles' might.

Labor 5 – The Augean Stables

The fifth labor of Heracles, as commanded by King Eurystheus, was a task that seemed mundane on the surface, yet it was laced with a challenge that tested the limits of endurance and ingenuity. Heracles was tasked to clean the Augean Stables, home to a vast number of divine cattle, which had not been cleaned for decades, if not centuries. These stables belonged to King Augeas, who possessed immense herds, and the accumulation of manure over the years had created a situation of unbearable filth and squalor.

Unlike his previous labors, this task was less about battling fearsome creatures and more about overcoming a seemingly impossible feat of cleansing and restoration. It was a labor that some might have deemed unworthy of a hero of Heracles' stature, yet it carried its own form of Herculean challenge.

Upon arriving at the kingdom of Augeas, Heracles proposed a bargain to the king. He would clean the stables in a single day, a feat that seemed beyond human capability, in exchange for a portion of the king's cattle. Augeas, incredulous and certain of the task's impossibility, agreed, unaware of Heracles' divine lineage and his reputation for accomplishing the unachievable.

Heracles, assessing the monumental task before him, devised a plan that relied more on wit than on physical strength. Instead of shoveling the waste, he diverted the courses of two nearby rivers, the Alpheus and the Peneus. He broke the walls of the stables and channeled the waters through them, turning the rivers into a makeshift cleansing torrent. The force of the water flushed out the stables, sweeping away years of accumulated filth, and leaving them in a pristine state.

In a single day, as promised, Heracles accomplished what would have taken ordinary men years to achieve. However, the success of this labor was marred by a subsequent dispute. King Augeas, reneging on his promise, refused to reward Heracles, arguing that the task had been accomplished through trickery rather than physical labor. This breach of agreement would later lead to a deeper conflict between Heracles and Augeas.

Labor 6 – The Stymphalian Birds

The sixth labor of Heracles, as assigned by King Eurystheus, required the hero to confront a peculiar and menacing challenge: the

Stymphalian Birds. These were no ordinary birds; they were malevolent creatures with beaks, claws, and wings of bronze, and their feathers could be launched as deadly, sharp projectiles. Dwelling in the swampy lake of Stymphalus in Arcadia, these birds were a scourge upon the land, destroying crops, livestock, and even humans.

The task of driving away or destroying these fearsome birds was daunting, as their habitat – the marshes around Lake Stymphalus – was nearly impenetrable, and the birds themselves were elusive and lethal. The inhospitable, murky terrain made direct confrontation risky and complicated, requiring a strategy that was both innovative and effective.

In this seemingly insurmountable endeavor, Heracles received assistance from Athena, the goddess of wisdom and war. Athena provided him with a pair of bronze krotala, clappers or noisemakers, crafted by the god Hephaestus. These were no ordinary instruments; their clanging was so piercing and cacophonous that it could startle and frighten even the most fearsome creatures.

Armed with these divine krotala, Heracles approached the swampy domain of the Stymphalian Birds. As he neared the lake, the ominous flapping of the birds' metallic wings and their shrill cries filled the air, creating a symphony of dread. Undeterred, Heracles climbed to a vantage point and began to clash the krotala with all his might. The sound was so thunderous and unbearable that it set the birds into a frenzy, causing them to take flight in a state of panic and confusion.

Seizing the moment, Heracles drew his bow and, with his unerring aim, shot arrow after arrow, each tipped with the lethal poison of the Lernaean Hydra. One by one, the Stymphalian Birds fell from the sky, their reign of terror brought to a swift and decisive end.

Labor 7 – The Cretan Bull

The seventh labor of Heracles, as commanded by King Eurystheus, led the hero to the island of Crete, a land ruled by the wise and powerful King Minos. Here, Heracles faced the task of capturing the Cretan Bull, an animal of immense strength and formidable temperament. This was no ordinary bull; it was a magnificent beast, sired by Poseidon himself, initially intended as a sacrifice to the god but spared by Minos, an act that would later lead to dire consequences.

The Cretan Bull was renowned across the land for its wild rampages. Its breath was said to blaze like fire, and its hooves carved deep furrows in the earth as it thundered across the countryside. The bull's capture was a task that tested more than brute strength; it required a strategic approach to subdue such a powerful and unpredictable creature.

Upon arriving in Crete, Heracles set about tracking the bull. He traversed the island's varied landscapes, from sun-drenched beaches to shadow-draped forests, following the trail of destruction left by the bull. The locals, who had long suffered under the bull's rampages, watched in a mixture of awe and skepticism. Many had tried to capture or kill the beast, and all had failed.

Heracles finally confronted the bull in a wide, open plain, where the creature charged at him with a fury that shook the ground. The hero met the charge head-on, grappling with the bull in a display of raw physical might. The struggle was titanic, a battle of strength and will between man and beast.

In a demonstration of his legendary prowess, Heracles overpowered the bull, wrestling it to the ground and subduing it without causing any harm. He then hoisted the bull upon his shoulders and began the journey back to Mycenae, a feat that stunned all who witnessed it.

Labor 8 – The Mares of Diomedes

The eighth labor of Heracles, as dictated by King Eurystheus, propelled the hero into a perilous venture steeped in danger and brutality. He was tasked with capturing the Mares of Diomedes, a quartet of wild, flesh-eating horses possessed of a savage and uncontrollable nature. These mares were not mere beasts of burden; they were the terrifying offspring of the gods, owned by Diomedes, the barbaric king of the Bistones of Thrace, a man as cruel and fierce as the animals he kept.

The mares - Podargos, Lampon, Xanthos, and Deinos - were infamous across the land for their viciousness. They were kept tethered to a bronze manger by chains, for no ordinary binding could hold them. Their diet of human flesh, fed to them by their merciless master Diomedes, only heightened their ferocity and made approaching them a near-suicidal endeavor.

As Heracles set foot in the land of the Bistones, he was met with hostility and suspicion. Undeterred, he formulated a plan to capture the mares, a scheme that required both stealth and immense physical prowess. Heracles initially attempted to take the mares by force, overpowering the guards and breaking the chains that bound the beasts.

The task, however, was complicated by the Bistonians, led by King Diomedes himself, who attacked Heracles in an effort to protect the famed horses. In the ensuing melee, Heracles called upon his companion, Abderus, to guard the mares while he dealt with the onslaught. The mares, however, overpowered the young Abderus, tragically killing him.

Enraged and grieved by the loss of his companion, Heracles returned to confront the mares. In a twist of poetic justice, he fed Diomedes to his own horses. This act of retribution had a profound effect: consuming their master calmed the mares, stripping them of their insatiable bloodlust.

The mares themselves, after being presented to Eurystheus, were eventually released. According to some versions of the myth, they were set free and roamed wild until their eventual deaths, no longer the man-eating monsters they had been under King Diomedes. In other accounts, they were given a more peaceful end, either by being given to Hera or by being set among the stars as a constellation.

Labor 9 – The Belt of Hippolyta

The ninth labor of Heracles, as commanded by King Eurystheus, plunged the hero into the heart of a tale woven with valor, deceit, and the complexities of divine interplay. Heracles was tasked with obtaining the belt of Hippolyta, the queen of the Amazons. This belt was not a mere piece of attire but a symbol of power and authority, given to Hippolyta by Ares, the god of war.

The Amazons were a tribe of warrior women, renowned for their skill in battle and their exclusion of men from their society. The prospect of venturing into their territory was daunting, for they were as formidable in combat as they were fierce in their independence.

As Heracles set sail for the land of the Amazons, his mind was a tumult of strategy and caution. Upon his arrival, he was met with a reception that was unexpectedly cordial. Hippolyta, intrigued by the reputation of Heracles and impressed by his prowess, welcomed him. The myths diverge at this point, offering different narratives of the ensuing events.

In one version, Hippolyta was so taken by the strength and heroism of Heracles that she agreed to give him her belt willingly. However, Hera, ever the antagonist in Heracles' labors, intervened. Disguised as an Amazon, she spread a rumor that Heracles intended to kidnap Hippolyta. This deceit incited the Amazons to arms, leading to a fierce battle. In the chaos, Heracles, believing Hippolyta had betrayed him, slew her, took the belt, and fought his way back to his ship.

Another version suggests that Heracles, anticipating hostility, kidnapped Hippolyta and demanded the belt as her ransom. Upon securing the belt, he released Hippolyta and departed, leaving the land of the Amazons behind.

Regardless of the narrative, the acquisition of Hippolyta's belt was a labor steeped in complexity and moral ambiguity.

Labor 10 – The Cattle of Geryon

The tenth labor of Heracles, as decreed by King Eurystheus, sent the hero on a journey to the far western edge of the world, to the island of Erytheia, where he was tasked with the formidable challenge of capturing the Cattle of Geryon. This labor was not just a test of strength but also of endurance and determination, as it required Heracles to travel farther than he had ever ventured before.

Geryon, the owner of the cattle, was a fearsome figure in his own right. He was a giant with three bodies, three heads, and an immense strength that matched his monstrous form. The cattle themselves were no ordinary herd; they were magnificent, red-hued, and guarded by Orthrus, a two-headed dog, brother to the infamous Cerberus, and the herdsman Eurytion.

Heracles' journey to Erytheia was an odyssey filled with trials and adventures. He journeyed through vast and uncharted lands, facing numerous obstacles along the way. In one notable episode, as he passed through the desert of Libya, he was so frustrated by the scorching heat that he shot an arrow at Helios, the sun god. Admiring the hero's boldness, Helios granted Heracles a golden cup, a vessel large enough to sail in, which Heracles used to reach Erytheia.

Upon arriving at the island, Heracles immediately set about completing his task. He first killed the fearsome Orthrus with a single blow of his club, a strike so swift and powerful that it caught the beast by surprise. Next, he dealt with Eurytion, the herdsman, dispatching him in a similar manner.

The confrontation with Geryon came next. Geryon, enraged by the death of his dog and herdsman, engaged Heracles in a fierce battle. It was a clash of titans, each blow from Geryon met with the indomitable strength of Heracles. In the end, Heracles slew Geryon with a volley of arrows, including those dipped in the lethal poison of the Lernaean Hydra.

With Geryon defeated, Heracles rounded up the cattle and began the arduous task of driving them back to Eurystheus. This journey back was as eventful as his journey to Erytheia, marked by various challenges and incidents. Heracles faced attacks from tribes and had to navigate difficult terrain, all while keeping the unruly cattle in check.

After many trials and tribulations, Heracles finally delivered the cattle to Eurystheus, completing his tenth labor.

Labor 11 – The Apples of the Hesperides

The eleventh labor of Heracles, as commanded by King Eurystheus, was a task that would take him to the edges of the known world and into the realm of gods and immortals. He was charged with the daunting mission of retrieving the Golden Apples of the Hesperides. These were not ordinary fruits but divine creations of golden radiance, gifts from Gaia to Hera at her marriage to Zeus, and were guarded by the Hesperides, nymphs of the evening, in a far-off garden at the western edge of the world. Adding to the peril, a fierce, hundred-headed dragon named Ladon, offspring of Phorcys and Ceto, watched over both the nymphs and the apples.

The journey to the Garden of the Hesperides was shrouded in mystery, as its exact location was a secret known to few. Heracles set out on a long and arduous journey, seeking guidance and information from various beings, both mortal and divine. His quest took him through many lands and presented numerous challenges, testing his resolve and strength.

One of the key moments in this labor occurred when Heracles, in his wanderings, encountered the Titan Prometheus. As an enduring consequence of his act of defiance in stealing fire from the gods and giving it to humanity, Prometheus was bound to a rock (or, in some versions, a mountain) in the Caucasus. Every day, an eagle, sent by Zeus, would arrive to feast on Prometheus' liver. Prometheus, being an immortal Titan, possessed the ability to regenerate his liver each night. Thus, his punishment was not only severe but also eternal in nature, as he was condemned to undergo this excruciating cycle of regeneration and consumption every day.

In an act of compassion and bravery, Heracles slew the eagle that tormented Prometheus, freeing the Titan from his eternal punishment. In gratitude, Prometheus offered Heracles valuable knowledge, including the location of the Garden of the Hesperides and the insight that Heracles could not retrieve the apples himself but would need the aid of Atlas, the Titan who held up the sky and who was the father of the Hesperides.

Heracles sought out Atlas and struck a bargain with him. He agreed to take on the burden of holding up the sky while Atlas fetched the apples. Atlas, relieved to be free of his burden, even temporarily, agreed and retrieved the apples from his daughters. However, upon his return, Atlas was reluctant to resume his duty. Heracles, cunningly, asked Atlas to hold the sky for just a moment so he could adjust his cloak for the weight. As soon as Atlas took back the sky, Heracles picked up the apples and set off on his return journey to Mycenae.

Labor 12 – Cerberus

The twelfth and final labor of Heracles, a task that would culminate his long and arduous journey of redemption, was perhaps the most perilous and profound of all. King Eurystheus commanded Heracles to descend into the Underworld – the realm of Hades, the god of the dead – and capture Cerberus, the fearsome three-headed dog who guarded its gates. This labor was not just a test of strength and courage but also a venture into the very heart of death and darkness.

Cerberus, the offspring of Typhon and Echidna, was a monstrous hound with three heads, each head harboring a set of snarling, razor-sharp teeth. His tail was said to be a serpent, and his back was lined with the heads of menacing snakes. To capture such a beast was a seemingly impossible feat, for no mortal had ever ventured into the Underworld and returned.

Heracles, undeterred by the daunting nature of his task, began his descent. Guided by Hermes, the messenger god, and Athena, the goddess of wisdom and war, Heracles journeyed through the shadowy realms, encountering lost souls and witnessing the mysteries of the afterlife.

Upon reaching the gates of the Underworld, Heracles encountered Hades and respectfully asked for permission to take Cerberus to the surface. Hades agreed under the condition that Heracles subdue the beast without using any weapons. Heracles, relying on his extraordinary strength, wrestled Cerberus and, using his lion-skin cloak to protect himself from the beast's venomous bites, managed to overpower and capture him.

Emerging from the Underworld with Cerberus in tow was a symbol of triumph over death itself, a feat that solidified Heracles' status as a hero of unparalleled prowess. The sight of the legendary hero, dragging the dreaded guardian of the Underworld into the light of day, was awe-inspiring and terrifying.

Upon presenting Cerberus to Eurystheus, Heracles had completed his final labor. The king, terrified at the sight of the fearsome beast, begged Heracles to return Cerberus to the Underworld. Heracles obliged, releasing Cerberus back into the care of Hades.

The Redemption of Heracles

Upon the completion of the Twelve Labors, Heracles had not only fulfilled the harsh decree of King Eurystheus but also redeemed himself for the tragic events that had set him on this perilous path. The successful conclusion of these daunting tasks marked a significant turning point in Heracles' life, both in terms of his personal redemption and his status as a mythological hero.

Firstly, the completion of the labors absolved Heracles of the guilt associated with the murder of his wife and children, a crime instigated by Hera's curse. This act of atonement was crucial in the ancient world, where the purification from miasma, or spiritual pollution caused by wrongdoing, was essential for restoring one's place in society and the natural order.

Secondly, Heracles' unparalleled success in these labors elevated him to an almost divine status. He had faced and overcome challenges that were not merely physical trials but also involved elements of cunning, endurance, and resilience against supernatural forces. His feats captured the collective imagination of the Greek world, establishing him as a paragon of strength, bravery, and virtue. The completion of the labors solidified his place in the pantheon of Greek heroes and greatly enhanced his reputation.

Following the labors, Heracles embarked on many other adventures and undertakings, further adding to his legend. He became involved in various quests and exploits, often helping gods and mortals alike. Some of his post-labor exploits included aiding the gods in the battle against the Giants (the Gigantomachy), participating in the Argonauts' quest for the Golden Fleece, and even inadvertently creating the Milky Way galaxy.

Heracles' life after the labors was not without its struggles and tragedies, however. He continued to face challenges and conflicts, some stemming from Hera's enduring hatred and others from the typical machinations of the heroic narrative. His mortal life eventually ended, but according to mythology, upon his death, he was granted immortality and ascended to Olympus, where he reconciled with Hera and married Hebe, the goddess of youth.

Chapter 7: Echo and Narcissus

The tale of Echo and Narcissus, steeped in themes of unrequited love and tragic self-obsession, is one of the more poignant and enduring stories in Greek mythology. It is a narrative that intertwines the lives of a loquacious nymph and a beautiful youth, culminating in a profound exploration of desire, rejection, and the consequences of vanity.

Echo was a vivacious and talkative nymph, known for her delightful conversation and her tendency to have the last word in every discussion. She caught the ire of Hera, the queen of the gods, with her loquacity. Hera was searching for her husband, Zeus, who was known for his numerous affairs with nymphs and mortals alike. To protect Zeus, Echo would engage Hera in long-winded conversations, giving Zeus time to escape. When Hera discovered this deceit, she cursed Echo, robbing her of her voice except for the ability to repeat the last words spoken to her.

Narcissus, on the other hand, was a young man of extraordinary beauty, admired and desired by many. However, he was aloof and disdainful, showing little interest in the affections directed towards him. His beauty was such that those who saw him often fell deeply in love with him, but Narcissus rejected all romantic advances, leaving a trail of despondent admirers in his wake.

Echo, upon seeing Narcissus wandering in the forest, was immediately captivated by his beauty and grace. She followed him, longing to speak to him, but hindered by Hera's curse, she was unable to initiate conversation. The opportunity arose when Narcissus, having become separated from his hunting companions, called out, "Is anyone there?" Echo, seizing her chance, repeated his words.

Drawn by the repeating voice, Narcissus called out again, and Echo responded in kind, her words a mere echo of his. Eventually, Echo revealed herself, hoping to embrace Narcissus, but he spurned her advances, leaving her heartbroken. Echo, consumed by her unrequited love and unable to express her grief due to the curse, wasted away, her body turning to stone. All that remained was her voice, which continued to echo in the lonely mountains and valleys.

Narcissus' rejection of Echo did not go unnoticed by the gods. Nemesis, the goddess of retribution, decided to punish Narcissus for his vanity and indifference. She lured him to a clear, still pool of water, where he caught sight of his reflection for the first time. Unaware that it was merely an image, Narcissus fell deeply in love with the beautiful figure he saw in the water. He became utterly entranced, unable to leave the captivating reflection. His obsession was so consuming that he eventually realized the futility of his love, leading to despair.

Unable to tear himself away from his reflection and tormented by unattainable love, Narcissus slowly withered away at the water's edge. In the place where he died, a flower sprang up, bearing his name – the narcissus.

Chapter 8: Prometheus Steals Fire

Prometheus, whose name means "forethought," was a Titan known for his wily intelligence and sympathy towards humans, whom he had helped create from clay at Zeus's command. While the other gods were aloof from human affairs, Prometheus showed a particular interest in their well-being and development.

The conflict between Prometheus and Zeus, the king of the gods, began at Mecone (later Sicyon), where a sacrificial meal was to determine the portions allocated to gods and humans. Prometheus, tasked with the division, cleverly butchered an ox and divided it into two portions. In one, he concealed the meat and edible parts inside the ox's stomach, an unappetizing exterior. In the other, he wrapped the bones in glistening fat, making it appear deceptively appealing. Zeus, knowing the deceit but choosing to play along, selected the fat-covered bones, thus determining that humans would keep the meat for themselves and burn the bones and fat as offerings to the gods.

Zeus, angered by Prometheus's trickery, retaliated by withholding fire from humanity, plunging them into cold and darkness, a state where survival and advancement were impossible. Prometheus, pained by the plight of humans, decided to act. He ascended to Olympus and stole fire from the hearth of the gods, concealing it in a hollow fennel stalk. He then brought this fire to humans, enabling them to warm themselves, cook food, forge metal, and harness the power for various arts and crafts. This gift of fire symbolized the dawn of civilization, the spark of creativity and knowledge that would define human existence.

Zeus, infuriated by Prometheus's defiance, devised a severe punishment for the Titan. He ordered Hephaestus, the god of blacksmiths, to chain Prometheus to a rock on a mountain (often identified as Mount Caucasus). There, Prometheus was to endure an eternal torment: each day, an eagle (or, in some versions, a vulture) would arrive to feast on his liver, which would regenerate each night, only to be consumed again the next day. This gruesome punishment was a symbol of Zeus's authority and a warning against defying the divine order.

Prometheus's suffering continued for years, a testament to his enduring spirit and the price of his rebellion. According to later traditions, he was eventually freed by the hero Heracles (Hercules), who, during one of his labors, slew the eagle and released Prometheus from his chains, with Zeus's permission. This act of liberation was often seen as a reconciliation between the human and divine realms, with Prometheus's foresight being instrumental in later myths, including the events leading to the Trojan War.

Chapter 9: Pandora's Box

The myth of Pandora's Box is one of the most intriguing and enduring tales in Greek mythology, encapsulating themes of curiosity, disobedience, and the unforeseen consequences of human actions. It is a story about the origins of human misfortune and the introduction of hope into the world.

The tale begins with the Titan Prometheus, who had incurred the wrath of Zeus, the king of the gods, by stealing fire from Olympus and giving it to humanity. To punish humanity for this transgression, Zeus devised a plan. He commanded Hephaestus, the god of craftsmanship, to create a woman of unparalleled beauty from clay. Each god and goddess bestowed upon this woman a unique gift, crafting her to be irresistible to men. Athena clothed her, Aphrodite gave her beauty, and Hermes, the messenger god, endowed her with cunning and deceitful words. This woman was named Pandora, which means "all-gifted," reflecting the many gifts she had received from the gods.

As part of her dowry, Pandora was given a pithos, often mistranslated as a 'box,' but was actually a large jar or storage vessel. She was warned by the gods never to open it. Pandora was then given in marriage to Epimetheus, the brother of Prometheus. Despite Prometheus's warning to his brother not to accept gifts from Zeus, Epimetheus was captivated by Pandora's beauty and welcomed her.

Curiosity, as it often does, got the better of Pandora. Despite the warnings, her curiosity about the contents of the jar grew more intense each day. Eventually, she could resist no longer. Pandora opened the jar, and from it escaped all the evils that would henceforth plague humanity – sickness, death, turmoil, strife, jealousy, hatred, famine, and all other miseries. The world, once a paradise, was now filled with suffering and sorrow.

Realizing what she had done, Pandora hastened to close the jar, but it was too late. All its contents had escaped, except for one thing that lay at the bottom – Hope. It is said that Zeus had included Hope in the jar as the only force that could make life bearable in the face of the hardships unleashed upon the world.

Chapter 10: The Abduction of Persephone

The story of the abduction of Persephone is a central myth in Greek mythology, rich in symbolism and themes of change, cyclical renewal, and the interplay between life and death. It is a tale that explains the changing seasons and underscores the ancient Greeks' understanding of the natural world.

Persephone, also known as Kore, was the daughter of Zeus and Demeter, the goddess of the harvest and fertility. Persephone was a beautiful and gentle young goddess, often depicted as the embodiment of spring's bounty and youth. She spent her days roaming the fields and meadows, delighting in the beauty of the natural world, surrounded by nymphs and the laughter of her companions.

Hades, the god of the Underworld, was struck by Persephone's beauty and grace during one of her excursions. Overcome with desire, he sought the permission of Zeus to marry her. Zeus, knowing that Demeter would never agree to her daughter's union with the somber lord of the dead, consented without Demeter's knowledge.

One day, as Persephone was gathering flowers, the earth suddenly split open, and Hades emerged in his dark chariot, drawn by immortal horses. In a swift and terrifying moment, he seized Persephone and carried her off to his realm, the Underworld, as the earth closed behind them, leaving no trace of the abduction.

Demeter, upon discovering her daughter's disappearance, was stricken with profound grief. She roamed the earth in search of Persephone, neglecting her duties as the goddess of the harvest. As a result, the earth ceased to be fertile; crops failed, and famine spread across the land. In her despair, Demeter withdrew her gifts from the world, and life began to wither.

The suffering of humanity eventually compelled Zeus to intervene. He sent Hermes, the messenger god, to the Underworld to retrieve Persephone. However, before Persephone left the Underworld, Hades offered her pomegranate seeds, the food of the dead. Unaware of the consequences, Persephone ate a few seeds.

According to the ancient laws, eating the food of the Underworld meant that Persephone was bound to it. As a result, a compromise was reached: Persephone would spend part of the year (usually one-third or half) with Hades in the Underworld and the rest with her mother on Olympus.

The myth of Persephone's abduction and return symbolizes the cycle of the seasons. Her time in the Underworld corresponds to the barren months of autumn and winter, when Demeter mourns and the earth lies dormant. Persephone's return to the surface world marks the arrival of spring and summer, as Demeter rejoices and the earth becomes fertile and fruitful once again.

In the Underworld, Persephone grew into her role as queen, becoming a figure of solemn dignity and power. She came to embody the dual aspects of life and death, renewal and decay. She was revered as a goddess of vegetation and a deity who offered guidance to the souls of the dead.

Chapter 11: Theseus and the Minotaur

The story of Theseus and the Minotaur is one of the most famous and thrilling tales from Greek mythology, intertwining elements of adventure, heroism, and the overcoming of monstrous adversity. It is set against the backdrop of ancient Athens and the island of Crete.

The tale begins with King Minos of Crete, who prayed to Poseidon, the sea god, for a sign of support for his claim to the throne. Poseidon sent a magnificent white bull, which Minos was supposed to sacrifice in the god's honor. However, Minos, awestruck by the beauty of the bull, decided to keep it and sacrificed another bull instead. Angered by this act of disobedience, Poseidon cursed Minos' wife, Queen Pasiphae, causing her to fall in love with the white bull. From their union, the Minotaur, a creature with the body of a man and the head of a bull, was born.

Ashamed and horrified, King Minos ordered the famous craftsman Daedalus to build a labyrinth - a vast, complex maze from which escape was impossible - to house the Minotaur. The creature was fed with human sacrifices, specifically youths from Athens.

This gruesome tribute stemmed from an earlier conflict where Minos' son Androgeos was killed in Athens. To avenge his son's death, Minos waged war and won. As punishment, Athens had to send seven young men and seven young women to Crete every nine years to be devoured by the Minotaur.

Theseus, the son of Aegeus, the king of Athens, was aghast at this cruel tribute. When the third sacrifice approached, he volunteered to be one of the seven youths with the aim of killing the Minotaur and ending the terror. His father, Aegeus, reluctantly agreed, extracting a promise from Theseus that if he survived, he would return with white sails instead of the customary black, signaling his victory.

Upon arriving in Crete, Theseus caught the eye of Ariadne, King Minos' daughter. She fell deeply in love with him. Knowing the fate that awaited Theseus, Ariadne approached Daedalus for help. Daedalus gave her a ball of thread and instructed her to give it to Theseus, advising him to tie one end at the entrance of the labyrinth and unwind it as he went deeper, so he could find his way back.

Armed with the thread and a sword, Theseus entered the labyrinth. He navigated the twisting, confusing paths, eventually encountering the Minotaur. In a fierce battle within the dark confines of the maze, Theseus used his strength and agility to slay the beast, ending its reign of terror. Following the thread back, he escaped the labyrinth with the other Athenians.

Theseus and his companions, along with Ariadne, who had helped him and now sought to flee with him, set sail for Athens. However, on the island of Naxos, Theseus either abandoned Ariadne or lost her, depending on the version of the myth. There are various accounts of what happened to Ariadne; in some, she was consoled by Dionysus, the god of wine, and married him.

Tragically, in the joy of his success and the grief of losing Ariadne, Theseus forgot to change the sails from black to white. Aegeus, anxiously watching for Theseus' return from a cliff overlooking the sea, saw the black sails and presumed his son was dead. In his despair, Aegeus threw himself into the sea, which was thereafter named the Aegean Sea in his memory.

Theseus' return to Athens was bittersweet. He had achieved a great heroic feat by defeating the Minotaur and had proven himself a worthy hero and future king. However, the victory was marred by the loss of his father and the complex emotions surrounding Ariadne's fate.

Chapter 12: Daedalus and Icarus

The story of Daedalus and Icarus is a poignant tale from Greek mythology that intertwines themes of genius, ambition, and the tragic consequences of hubris. It is a narrative rich in symbolism, often interpreted as a cautionary tale about the limits of human innovation and the dangers of overreaching.

Daedalus was renowned throughout the ancient world for his extraordinary skill as an inventor, architect, and craftsman. His creations were not only beautiful but also marvels of ingenuity and engineering. However, his life was marked by both triumph and tragedy, often a result of his own talents and decisions.

One of Daedalus' most famous creations was the labyrinth on the island of Crete, a complex and bewildering maze built to house the Minotaur, the monstrous offspring of Pasiphae, the wife of King Minos, and a magnificent bull. The labyrinth was so ingeniously designed that no one who entered could find their way out without guidance.

After Theseus, the prince of Athens, succeeded in killing the Minotaur with the help of Minos' daughter, Ariadne, Daedalus fell out of favor with King Minos. Some versions of the myth suggest that Minos was angered by Daedalus' involvement in the Minotaur's demise or other transgressions. As a result, Daedalus and his son Icarus were imprisoned in a tower on Crete to prevent Daedalus' knowledge of the labyrinth from spreading to the outside world.

Determined to escape and return to their homeland, Daedalus devised a plan to flee the island. Using his unparalleled skills, Daedalus constructed two sets of wings made from feathers and wax. He carefully arranged the feathers and secured them with wax, creating a pair of functional wings for himself and Icarus.

Before their flight, Daedalus warned Icarus of the dangers of complacency and hubris. He instructed his son not to fly too low, lest the dampness of the sea clog his wings, and not too high, lest the heat of the sun melt the wax. The middle path, he advised, was the safest.

The day of their escape arrived, and father and son donned their wings. They took off from the tower, soaring into the sky, a breathtaking sight to behold. For a time, they flew as Daedalus had planned, marveling at the feeling of freedom and the view of the world below.

However, Icarus, exhilarated by the thrill of flight and perhaps forgetting his father's warning, began to ascend higher and higher. He reveled in the experience, soaring towards the sun, unaware of the impending danger. As they neared the sun, the heat began to melt the wax in Icarus' wings. Despite Daedalus' frantic warnings, it was too late. The wings disintegrated, and Icarus plummeted from the sky, falling into the sea below, where he drowned.

Daedalus witnessed the tragic fall of his son with horror and grief. He continued his flight alone, eventually reaching the safety of land. Consumed by sorrow and guilt over the loss of Icarus, Daedalus lamented his part in the tragedy – his invention had enabled their escape but at a terrible cost.

Chapter 13: Perseus and the Gorgon Medusa

The story of Perseus and the Gorgon Medusa is one of the classic tales of Greek mythology, filled with monsters, gods, and heroism. It is the story of Perseus, one of the most celebrated heroes in Greek lore, and his quest to defeat Medusa, one of the three Gorgon sisters, whose gaze could turn anyone who looked directly at her into stone.

Perseus' story begins with his mother, Danaë, the daughter of King Acrisius of Argos. An oracle prophesied to Acrisius that Danaë's son would one day kill him. To prevent this, Acrisius imprisoned Danaë in a bronze chamber. However, Zeus, attracted by Danaë's beauty, visited her in the form of golden rain and impregnated her. Perseus was born from this union.

When Acrisius discovered the child, he cast Danaë and Perseus into the sea in a wooden chest to avoid directly killing them. The chest drifted to the island of Seriphos, where a fisherman named Dictys rescued and raised Perseus.

When Perseus reached adulthood, Polydectes, the king of Seriphos, who desired Danaë, planned to get rid of Perseus by sending him on an impossible mission: to bring back the head of Medusa. Medusa, once a beautiful maiden, had been cursed by Athena and transformed into a Gorgon, a creature with snakes for hair, whose gaze turned onlookers to stone.

Recognizing the peril of this quest, the gods decided to aid Perseus. Athena, the goddess of wisdom and war, provided him with a mirrored shield, while Hermes, the messenger god, gave him a pair of winged sandals for flight and a sickle to decapitate Medusa. Perseus also received a helm of darkness from Hades, which rendered its wearer invisible.

Perseus' first task was to find the Hesperides, the nymphs who possessed knowledge of Medusa's whereabouts. To locate them, he first had to seek the Graeae, sisters of the Gorgons, who shared a single eye and tooth among them. By seizing their eye and tooth, Perseus compelled them to reveal the location of the Hesperides.

The Hesperides, in turn, equipped Perseus with further knowledge and tools: a knapsack to safely contain Medusa's head and the location of the Gorgons.

Perseus reached the Gorgons' lair while they slept. Using the mirrored shield to view Medusa's reflection, he avoided her deadly gaze. He approached Medusa, invisible thanks to Hades' helm, and with a swift stroke of the sickle, decapitated her. From Medusa's neck sprang Pegasus, the winged horse, and Chrysaor, a giant wielding a golden sword, both fathered by Poseidon.

With Medusa's head in his knapsack, Perseus embarked on his return journey. Along the way, he encountered Andromeda, who was to be sacrificed to a sea monster. Perseus used Medusa's head to petrify the monster and rescued Andromeda, taking her as his wife.

Eventually, Perseus returned to Seriphos, where he found that his mother had been mistreated by Polydectes. He confronted the king and used Medusa's head to turn him to stone, thus liberating Danaë and the island.

Perseus and Danaë returned to Argos. However, mindful of the prophecy that he would kill his grandfather, Perseus stayed away from Acrisius. Ironically, the prophecy was fulfilled at a later athletic competition, where an errant discus thrown by Perseus struck and killed an elderly spectator, who turned out to be Acrisius.

Perseus' adventures did not end there, but his quest to slay Medusa remains his most famous exploit. After his various adventures, he eventually founded Mycenae and became one of the legendary kings of ancient Greece. Medusa's head was given to Athena, who placed it on her shield, the Aegis.

Chapter 14: King Midas and his Golden Touch

The story of King Midas and his golden touch is a well-known and enduring myth from Greek mythology, rich in themes of greed, consequence, and the understanding of true value. It serves as a cautionary tale about the dangers of excessive greed and the misjudgment of what constitutes true wealth and happiness.

Midas was the king of Phrygia, a region in Asia Minor, and was known for his wealth and also, according to some versions of the myth, his foolishness and lack of judgment. The most famous story about Midas is his wish for the ability to turn everything he touched into gold.

The story begins with Dionysus, the god of wine, festivity, and ecstatic celebration. One day, Silenus, a companion and tutor to Dionysus, became intoxicated and was found by some of Midas' men in the king's rose garden. Instead of punishing him, Midas treated Silenus with kindness and hospitality, entertaining him for several days. When he returned Silenus to Dionysus, the god, grateful for Midas' hospitality, offered him a wish of his choosing.

Midas, already a man of great wealth, made a wish that revealed his true avarice. He asked that everything he touched turn to gold. Dionysus, perhaps perceiving the folly in this request, nonetheless granted Midas his wish, warning him about the dangers of his desire.

At first, Midas was overjoyed with his new power. He turned twigs, stones, and even his roses into gold. However, his joy quickly turned to despair when he realized the grave consequences of his wish. When he embraced his daughter, she turned into a golden statue. His food and drink also turned to gold, rendering him unable to eat or drink.

Midas soon understood the curse of his "golden touch." Wealth, which he had valued above all else, became his greatest torment. In a state of anguish, he prayed to Dionysus, begging to be relieved of his power.

Dionysus, merciful and perhaps intending to teach Midas a lesson, heard his plea. He instructed Midas to wash in the river Pactolus, which would remove his cursed touch. Midas did as he was told, and as he bathed in the river, his power flowed into the waters, turning the river sands golden. This myth explains why the river Pactolus was historically rich in gold.

Having learned his lesson, Midas renounced his greed and devoted himself to a simpler, more humble life. In some versions of the myth, he became a follower of Pan or Dionysus, embracing the pleasures of nature and the countryside over material wealth.

Conclusion

As we close the pages of "Greek Mythology: A Collection of the Best Greek Myths," we reflect upon a journey that has taken us through the majestic realms of Titans and Olympians, into the depths of ancient creation myths, and across a spectrum of tales that have shaped much of Western narrative tradition. From the primordial chaos to the intricate labyrinth of Daedalus, from the lofty heights of Olympus to the sun-scorched encounter of Icarus with his fate, these stories offer more than just a glimpse into the ancient Greek psyche— they reveal universal truths about the human condition.

These enduring Greek myths have influenced art, literature, philosophy, and culture in innumerable ways, continuing to inspire and intrigue us. The gods and heroes of ancient Greece, with their complex personalities and dramatic stories, invite us to reflect on our own lives, our struggles, our triumphs, and our place in the world's ever-unfolding story.

I hope you have enjoyed this exploration into the world of Greek Mythology. If you would like to share your feedback, it is greatly appreciated if you could take a minute to leave us a review on Amazon. It really helps us to continue producing books that readers love!

And finally, if you liked this book, please keep an eye out for the other books in this series, also available for sale on Amazon as well as through many other online retailers. The other books in this series include:

- Roman Mythology: A Collection of the Best Roman Myths

- Norse Mythology: A Collection of the Best Norse Myths

- Egyptian Mythology: A Collection of the Best Egyptian Myths

- Celtic Mythology: A Collection of the Best Celtic Myths